Until They Have Faces

Stories of Recovery, Resilience, and Redemption

Photography by David M. Page
Compiled by Elle Page
Edited by Susan Deans

Photographs by: DMPage Images
Compiled by: Lynn Elle Page
Edited by: Susan Deans
Cover and book design by: Sue Campbell Graphic Design

ISBN: 978-0-615-57095-2

Published by DMPage Images
            8461 Pawnee Lane
            Niwot, Colorado 80503
Printed in the United States of America

"We know about poor people.
It's the poor people we don't know."
— Mother Teresa

The Backstory

The homeless. Such a simple label conjures a host of pictures, assumptions and judgments in our minds. For some it's, "They're all alcoholics and addicts." For others, it's, "Why don't they just get a job!"

Biases are well-researched phenomena. We challenge our negative biases best when we spend time with individuals from the stereotypical group. Getting a more complete, more educated picture can significantly transform our initial set of assumptions and beliefs. My husband, David, and I experienced this on October 16, 2010.

As a new advisory board member for Project Revive: Boulder, I volunteered for its first community project, cleaning the Boulder Creek corridor, location of numerous homeless camping areas. We were to work side-by-side with other volunteers, some of them homeless or formerly homeless. I asked David to join me and document the event photographically.

As we walked and worked with members of Boulder's homeless population that day, we learned of the wide variety of life experiences and circumstances that had brought them to such a low point in their lives and why they had volunteered for the cleanup project. Our stereotypes were challenged. We left inspired and

> In a January 2009 survey there were 1,050 homeless individuals and family members in Boulder.
> —National Point in Time survey, January 2009

changed. We drove home that day debriefing our extraordinary experience and David shared his vision for this book.

For the next year, David captured the portraits that follow in these pages and I coordinated a team of writers to capture the stories behind the faces. All of us who have participated in this book have grown and been nourished through our personal interactions with these largely invisible people. And the homeless we've met have tasted the dignity of being central to a larger purpose as we listened, recorded, photographed and captured their lives as reflected in these portraits and pages.

Through *Until They Have Faces*, we introduce you to individuals who are or have been homeless in Boulder, Colorado, and to the people and places in the larger society with whom they regularly "intersect." We hope that these pictures and stories will answer many of the questions you'd like to ask but don't, and that your assumptions and beliefs will be challenged, too.

Thank you for inviting the homeless into your home through this book. They won't be fully understood and loved until they have faces.

—Elle Page

The Context

The project's volunteer writers were asked to give voice to the people you'll meet in this book, to help them communicate whatever message they chose. The authors heard stories about how people became homeless, how they view their lives, the prejudice they encounter and their dreams for the future. These stories are meant to be unique, not necessarily consistent with each other or formulaic — just what the interviewer/writer experienced.

In preparation for their interviews, our writers were told they would encounter people who have experienced extreme trauma, are dealing with post-traumatic stress disorder, have physical and mental illnesses, addictions and/or are recovering from addictions. In our effort to address the individuals respectfully and in consideration of these issues, you may notice holes in the stories, unanswered questions or inconsistencies. Please read each story with this context in mind. These are unique individuals expressing their reality as honestly as they can, wanting to be seen the way they see themselves.

You will also notice no pictures of individuals under 18 — except for a boy pictured with his mother. This is not because Boulder has no children on its streets. There are many but they are not old enough to sign a release for photography, nor do they have guardians to do so, and to respect their privacy, none are included. To respect the privacy of all of our subjects only first names are used.

Several of the subjects in the book are now off the street and in housing. While this is clearly a positive step out of homelessness, it can be tenuous with the added responsibility for rent and associated housing costs. Those who have recently transitioned to housing are often still dependent on the support offered by the community.

While we in no way wanted to put rose-colored filters on the stories, we also chose not to give voice to pent-up vitriol or political positions. The intent of these stories is to be informative rather than persuasive; to break stereotypes and to make the invisible, visible.

Half of the homeless in Boulder County reported a disabling condition.
Serious mental illness — 31%
Substance abuse — 28%
Co-occurring disorders — 18%
Physical disability 17%
2009 PIT — Metropolitan Denver Homeless Initiative (MDHI)

The Proceeds

from this project will be distributed to:

Boulder Outreach for Homeless Overflow (BOHO)

Many in our community are unaware that the Boulder Shelter for the Homeless cannot offer shelter to the entire local homeless population on our cold winter nights.

On nights when the temperature is 38 degrees Fahrenheit with moisture, or 32 degrees with no moisture, Boulder Outreach for Homeless Overflow (BOHO) provides emergency warming centers in cooperation with a network of faith communities. Seven local churches and a synagogue open their doors on a rotating schedule that is well known among the city's homeless population. The overflow offers warm floor space for people who would otherwise be on the streets. In addition to the warming centers, BOHO sponsors The FEED (Friends Encouraging Eating Daily), which helps fill gaps in local meal services for the homeless, and Medical Respite Boulder, which fills gaps in medical care for the homeless. BOHO is a safety net for the safety net, seeking to fill service gaps in the context of community. BOHO is truly a homeless organization serving the homeless, with no office space or facilities of its own.

http://bohocommunity.com

The Bridge House

The Bridge House, formerly the Carriage House Community Table, is a valuable resource for Boulder's homeless population. People begin lining up well before its 9 a.m. weekday opening, eager for a cup of coffee or breakfast. The volunteers serve an average of 200 people daily.

A surprisingly wide variety of services are offered at this beacon of hope at 1120½ Pine Street in Boulder, tucked behind the First Congregational Church, and through associated churches. The homeless and working poor have the opportunity to receive hot meals (lunch five days a week and dinners at local churches three to four days a week), medical and mental health services. They can meet with case managers who will assist them with everything from employment services to addiction concerns.

A licensed social worker conducts weekly addiction recovery groups. Twice a week a staff member from the Boulder Mental Health Center is on-site, once a week a professional from Clinica Family Health Services is available, and a holistic health clinic offering acupuncture is available once a week.

The Bridge House provides free voice mail for job seekers, individual tutoring, assistance in preparing resumes, interview clothing and computer access.

www.boulderbridgehouse.org

The Men

Men comprise the majority of the homeless population. The twenty-six who shared their stories disclose a spectrum of backgrounds and views on their situation.

Mark S.

by Elle Page

I could see the wariness in their eyes as we approached their camp on a less-traveled path in the woods along the Boulder Creek. It helped that we were with a well-known leader in the community who provides daily services to the homeless. Only one of the three men, Mark, was interested in being photographed and sharing his story. He stepped aside to talk with me, all of his 60 years written on his unshaven, weathered face with red-rimmed eyes.

Mark was eager to share; his story a precious keepsake as well as a source of shame. "I grew up helping that which I am now. My mother was Joan Sparks who ran the largest food bank in the country," he said with pride. "She has a plaque in the San Jose Rose Garden." He is overcome with emotion, the tears flow and he steps away. "When Vietnam refugees came to our city, my mom found sponsors for every one of them. I was there. And look where I am now." Again, the tears flow. "I should have done more than my mom."

A carefully packed, large pile of various bundles, his worldly possessions, sits on a well-engineered, wheeled rack at the edge of the camp. "I'm still working on it," he explains. "The key is in the curve of the sidepieces. The patent is not quite complete. I want to put a small aluminum plate and then it will be the ultimate packer,"

"I'm just trying to live like you. You need to open that heart. You need to dig. ..."

he adds with a swelling of his chest.

Mark's ultimate packer, which can be wheeled or carried, has served him well from Alaska to Florida. He has only recently arrived in Boulder. I tried to coax more of Mark's story from him. How did he get here? But he kept returning to the mother who set such an extraordinary example. "She was even a mediator between the Hell's Angels and the Black Panthers. We were peacekeepers. We were helpers. I live for peace yet look where I live now," his shame creeping back. "I'm looked at downward. How can that be?" More tears of grief.

Mark feels ashamed when people walk by him and judge him with a look, a gesture or yell unkind words. He has advice for us. "I'm just trying to live like you. You need to open that heart. You need to dig. If you keep living the angry, hatred way you are just going to destroy yourself."

My time with Mark and his heart's grip on his mother's story made me want to know more. "Look her up!" Mark had encouraged. A short Google search uncovered a story by Glen D. Kittler about this remarkable woman who ran away from an unhappy home at age 14.

"Joan's first husband and a son were killed in a car accident. They had been a circus family,

traveling constantly. Joan was an animal trainer and her husband was a magician. One night while on the road their van skidded on a soft shoulder and toppled. Joan and two other children survived.... In 1961, Joan married the chief mechanic with the circus."

It was through her new mother-in-law that Joan was introduced to "the peace of the Lord" that changed her life. *"She convinced her second husband that they should quit the circus, settle down, join a church, and raise their children in a stable home.... But in January, 1962 ... the lure of the road overpowered Joan's husband. He rejoined a circus, leaving her with two children and a third child on the way (Mark, born in July). Because she wasn't as yet a legal resident of the state, she did not qualify for welfare assistance. She was utterly stranded."*

Through determination, compassion and numerous miracles, Joan founded the Good Samaritan Home in Oakland, California, became an ordained minister, helped thousands of indigent women and children, served up to 10,000 meals a month and adopted 15 children in addition to her 3 natural ones. "They're probably all over the country now," reflected Mark with a sigh of loss.

Mark's heritage of compassion is in the phrases he repeats throughout our conversation: "Our biggest problem in this world is we're not social enough. Being able to walk up to a group, sit down, have a cup of coffee and," he says with emphasis, *"be a part of life. Communication is the key."*

He shifts back to his own role and current circumstances. "Every place in this world is sacred ... I want to do something good. I was supposed to go beyond her and I haven't done near enough."

"Paul"

by Kathy Kaiser

There's no doubt that Paul has had a hard life. He started doing drugs at age fourteen in Boulder where he grew up, and later served time in a state prison where he witnessed murders and almost died in an industrial accident. In Boulder, where he's been homeless for most of the time since 1998, he's been beaten by other homeless people and suffers from a rash of health problems. Nine weeks ago, doctors told him that he didn't have more than a year to live. Yet, at the time of our interview, he had been clean and sober for 58 days. His biography, he half jokes, should be called "Against All Odds."

During a period he describes as a normal life, Paul was married for 10 years and worked successfully as an audio-equipment salesman. But when his substance abuse returned and he and his wife grew apart, the marriage failed.

In his travels through several states, Paul bought heroin from an undercover policeman. Because the police believed he was a dealer, Paul was convicted of a felony. He was sentenced to 10 years, although he served five. In prison, he experienced riot situations, witnessed murders in which the guards participated, and stabbed another inmate who tried to rape him. While in a storage tank filled with corn (as part of a prison job) he was "buried alive." During the rescue, his back was broken, an injury that still affects his health.

By returning to Colorado he violated his parole, which means he's a wanted man and can't apply for Social Security, food stamps or assisted housing. Yet Paul uses the same skills that made him a top salesman to earn a living as a panhandler, making $25,000 a year. It's five times more than any other homeless person in Boulder makes, he claims, and he partly attributes his success to his flimsy cardboard sign: "Very clean and sober older person lost everything due to chronic illness. … In and out of the hospital. Desperate! Been very sick. Trying to raise $ for meds, bus fares, and special foods I need."

He succeeds also, he says, because "I appear to be like everyone else. I take a shower and clean up every day," sticks his long hair under his hat and dresses in good clothes.

Before getting off drugs and alcohol, "My body swelled up so badly I couldn't see my knuckles. My liver was shutting down and my pancreas was enlarged. I was hospitalized six times with acute pancreatitis, which is deadly." The doctors gave him a "death warrant" and told him there was no hope. Yet something in Paul made him want to fight back. He joined Alcoholics Anonymous (AA), got a membership in an athletic club, and enlisted the help of a nutritionist.

> His biography, he half jokes, should be called "Against All Odds."

"Paul"

In AA, Paul was told that he was in the worst physical and mental condition of anyone they had seen. A member of the Mennonite Church, he credits God with his turnaround. "God pulled me out of it. I believe in a power greater than me."

But every day is a struggle. He is in constant pain from his physical problems and feels confused and disoriented from the drug withdrawal. "I'm a wreck.... It's a miracle I don't do drugs because I'm exposed [to them] every day."

He's full of regrets for a life that should have been different. "If I weren't a drug addict, I'd have family, work in retail or be in some upper-management position, living someplace [nice]." Before his arrest, he worked as an attendant in a detox unit and once considered getting a license to be an addiction counselor. "But I never made that goal because of drugs and alcohol. ... Mentally, I'll never return to my normal marbles."

He describes his drug addiction as either genetic or learned personality but accepts responsibility for what he became. He remembers in 1980 in California seeing a homeless man. "I saw [that] I could be the guy pushing the shopping cart and going through the recycling bin. I saw the future ... but couldn't stop it."

Paul has no illusions about the future and how difficult his life will be. "I have to use every bit of my survival skills to stay off the street, because if I'm on the street I'll die. ... I'm not going to live a long time. ... I don't have a positive, rosy future. This is the very worst, hopeless situation a human can be in."

And yet, somehow, despite all his problems, Paul, now 56, does have hope. He says the daily AA meetings are "keeping me alive" and he's even thinking about buying a mobile home and going back to school. Against all odds, Paul is still standing.

Grant

Grant

by Mary Beth Lagerborg

Grant's clear blue eyes crinkle with mirth; they say he's open to conversation. He looks like a musician or an artist, although his story doesn't go down that path. But his education and his options seem to have ended early.

"I'm 28," Grant said, "and homeless for the fourth time. ...The first time was when I was 14. My parents said, 'Grant, we've had enough of you. You can't follow the rules. Get out.'

"I bummed around for a little bit, stayed with friends. But my friend's mom said I had to leave."

As Grant describes the years between 14 and 28, it feels like he's been blown in the wind. Kicked out of his grandmother's house for drinking too much. Tried nursing. Got a business up and running, then it slipped between his fingers.

"I've been learning along the way," Grant said. "The more you realize you can do, the more you are able to get out and make a change for yourself." But he has also discovered that once he became used to homelessness, it was easy to slide into it again.

His most successful venture was a business with his two brothers, gardening for medical marijuana, until a disagreement split them apart. "I did good," said Grant. "I had a car, an apartment, a girlfriend, a whole business life," until he tried dope. People tried to persuade him and he said "no," but finally he did try it.

"You try it and you're like, oh, it's wonderful. Before you know it, it's five dollars a day, 10 dollars a day, 15 dollars, 100 dollars, and then you're doing 250 dollars a day. You sell your car, your old coins, anything you've got."

After this, after he'd lost everything, Grant took care of an old man he calls Uncle Bob, although they're not related. Uncle Bob was too weak to walk even with a cane, smoked cigarettes constantly and his house was overrun with mice. "I felt sorry for this guy," said Grant. He had no one to take care of him, and Grant said that he learned patience listening to Bob tell the same stories over and over and caring for him.

Grant said he'd talked to Uncle Bob just the night before. "I actually lived there for a while," Grant said, but Uncle Bob asked him to go. "It was just like 'I need my space, you need yours. You're coming into your thirties and I'm coming into my seventies.'"

Grant's most recent stint of homelessness had just begun. He had left Uncle Bob's and was living with his brother. "I've been living with

> ... he has also discovered that once he became used to homelessness, it was easy to slide into it again.

15

him for about twelve days, until last night," Grant said. "You'd think I could stay. He's my brother."

When asked what Grant would like his life to look like, he said, "I would like normal life."

What is that, a "normal life?"

"A house, a business of mine that I get off the ground."

Grant doesn't know about a family. "I'm only 28," he said.

He wears a purple bracelet with these words on it: "patient," "reliable," "persistent," "determined." He said Uncle Bob gave him the bracelet. He thinks the bracelet is even nicer because he tries to think of himself as a very patient person most of the time.

"Life is what you expect out of it," Grant said.

Mark A.

by Jodi Burnett

Mark is a distinguished-looking and intelligent man with an ever-present sense of humor lurking behind every remark. He wears a back brace while he heals from two compression fractures he incurred in a fall on the Boulder Creek path. Otherwise, Mark looks like the guy next door. His life has been lived on the waves of history from the last half of the 20th Century until now.

Mark said he was born in Rockville Centre, N.Y., in 1950. His family moved to Amityville in 1958 and he graduated from the local high school in 1968. Mark was later drafted, he said, and served in the Army Security Agency during the Vietnam War. After surviving a mortar shell explosion and subsequent surgery, he said he returned home to America only to endure being cursed at and called a "baby killer" by the "Peace-Not-War" hippies. Soon after his return stateside, Mark got married and the couple had two daughters. He attempted to run a Phillips 66 gas station, only to be hit with the gas shortage of 1973. He then worked for Montgomery Ward before being recruited by IBM. With a rewarding electronic/mechanical design job on the cutting-edge of personal computers, working with hard disks and optical drives, he bought a new home and a new car. Life began to look pretty good to Mark, but not to his wife. Sadly, she

> He remembers being truly scared and thinking, "I'm not done yet!"

left him after 11 years of marriage, he said.

The affluent 1980s and 90s saw Mark living the high life. He remarried and eventually moved to Coal Creek. His career was rocketing and he enjoyed a six-figure income. There were a lot of friends and too much partying. Mark said he spent most of his spare time remodeling the house and began high-performance sailing. He even started his own boat company.

Mark's life began to tumble like a line of dominos in 2005. The stock market crashed and he lost his fortune and his business. With 24 years behind them, Mark and his second wife divorced. Around the same time, Mark was diagnosed with high blood pressure. Reacting in grief over the loss of his marriage, Mark started drinking, mixing alcohol with blood pressure medication. One night as he drove away from a Super Bowl party he had a heart attack and collapsed over the steering wheel of his truck. The truck was still in reverse when it crashed into a Cadillac Escalade, whose OnStar System alerted police. While they were on their way, he suffered a second heart attack. In the ambulance, lying on the gurney, Mark then had a small stroke. He remembers being truly scared and thinking, "I'm not done yet!"

Mark was diagnosed with a partially collapsed femoral artery and , he said, had to have emergency

Mark A.

bypass surgery. After his recovery he was sent to jail for the DUI. He was unable to make his mortgage payment and other payments, and his house went into foreclosure. When Mark was finally released from jail, he was homeless.

Asked what he thought people needed to understand about homelessness, Mark said, "Take a look at Japan, Chernobyl and the Twin Towers. … Lives can change like that!" He snapped his fingers. "You can't get insurance for that. All people are vulnerable. This could happen to anyone in a millisecond without notice." Mark finds his hope in the people around him. The other homeless people he knows in the community are very encouraging. He has also reconnected with a friend who lives in North Carolina, with whom he had spent his childhood and high school years.

As a boy, Mark loved to take apart and rebuild anything electronic or mechanical. He remembers being mesmerized by the Soviet satellite Sputnik and trying to build his own satellite out of old paint cans and a night light. Mark now holds degrees in both mechanical and electrical engineering, he said. Today Mark has some new irons in the fire. He still owns his creation, a product that makes septic systems more efficient. He hopes to sell it and use the proceeds to invest in the development of other inventions. In the future, Mark wants to give back to society by mentoring kids. He is working with the Carriage House Community Table on implementing a computer program that matches mentors and teachers with students who want to get their GEDs. Mark also loves to cook and is working with his friend, Lacey, to write a cookbook called *Cooking Intuitively*. Mark laughs. "I'm pulling it together. I'm not done yet!"

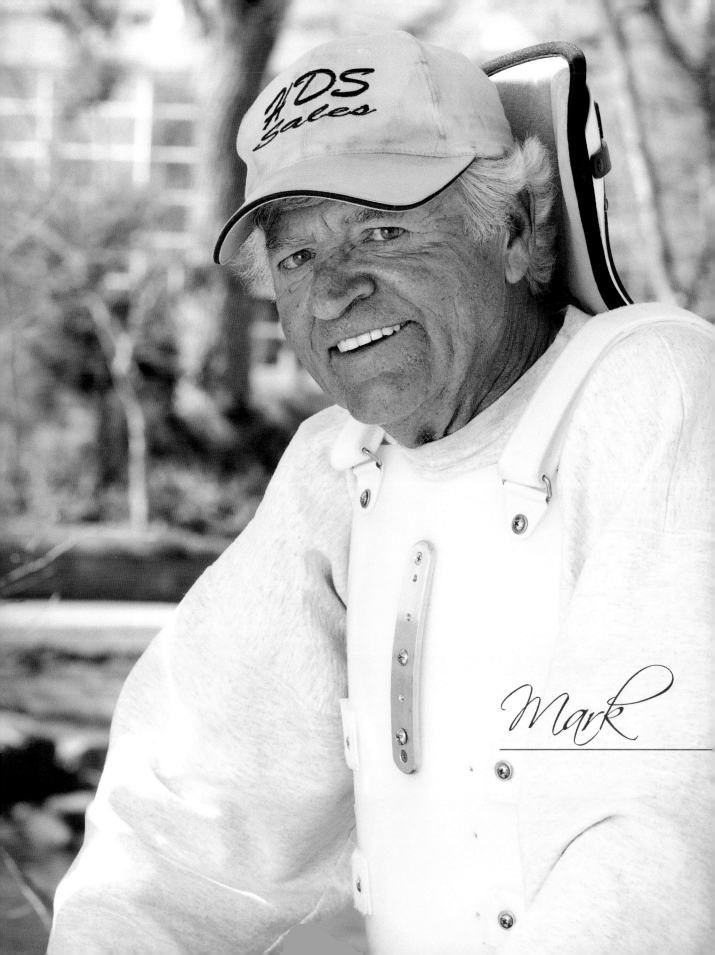

Mark

Chad

Chad

by Taylor Pappas

I met Chad on a bright, cold, overcast spring day. People strolled the Pearl Street Mall during their lunch breaks as I sat in a café.

When Chad walked through the door, he greeted me with a handshake and a grin. We bought coffee and took a seat next to the window overlooking the Pearl Street Mall.

Chad has incredible insight when it comes to the subject of homelessness because he is no longer a homeless man. However, Chad continues to help homeless people through his work. He has volunteered with a rescue mission in downtown Denver and currently is employed with the Carriage House Community Table in Boulder. Chad is also working to gain more certificates so that he can continue doing more social work.

Chad's early life was hard. He was abandoned at a fire station when he was 18 months old, he said. He was adopted but had conflicts with his adoptive family and left them in 1997 due to his drug and alcohol use.

As he described his experiences, it became clear that he enjoyed traveling while a homeless man. When he became accustomed to the environment where he was living, he often desired something new. His homelessness gave him a sense of freedom, in a way, yet he also felt deep isolation. Chad has encountered many different places, people and things – ranging from the streets of Boulder to the parks of San Francisco. He came to know places in ways that were unique to those homeless who lived there. He can identify safe places in the woods and places where food is available that others are unlikely to find. The idea of a rolling stone that gathers no moss comes to mind. "When things got too easy, I moved on," he said.

Chad enjoys the outdoors, especially fishing and camping, which have given him valuable skills for survival. In a way, being homeless was an experience with nature. By enduring the elements, he proved that he could survive in ways that not many can. Of course, being homeless had dangerous aspects: other people, the police and the elements all at times posed risk. Uncertainty about when he would have his next meal or where he would sleep for the night was always an issue, but he said it was nothing he could not overcome.

The time we spent talking that afternoon was enjoyable. Now sober 18 months, Chad is a charming and intelligent man, quick to respond to any question I had. He is a man with much valuable insight into the

> Chad sees the beauty in everyone, but is also aware of others' frailties and vulnerabilities.

world. We talked not only about how the homeless live, but also about the way a man who has experienced homelessness sees and interprets the world. The hustle and bustle of the people moving along the mall was enough for him to laugh and say, "People are robots."

Chad sees the beauty in everyone, but is also aware of others' frailties and vulnerabilities. He is compassionate but knows that people must want a different life in order to build one for themselves.

Chad's homelessness didn't make him desperate or broken from years on the streets. He has developed the perspective of a man who is empowered by the hardships and triumphs of his homeless past. He understands that life is more than a cell phone and a job. It is about *living*. And Chad will tell you he has done just that.

Steve C.

Steve C.
by Kate Guilford

Steve's future glowed brightly when he was a 22-year-old college senior with a 3.9 grade point average in electrical engineering. It crashed around him when his first fierce bout of mental illness forced him to drop out of college and return home. This began a lifelong challenge to find mental and physical stability.

After being homeless many times in several states over the last 30 years, Steve now lives in a Boulder apartment, is stable on his medications, pays his bills and stays out of trouble. He accomplished this with the help of the Maslin House Shelter Plus Care Program. "Without their help I'd still be homeless.... Now that I've graduated I don't go there any more except to see the psychiatrist and my therapist."

"For a while I went there every day to take my meds, and someone paid my bill. You graduate by behaving yourself and taking your meds like you're supposed to. After a while they think you can handle it on your own. I did that before, but I couldn't afford the medications, so I became manic again. ... I'm thankful that they got that Medicare Part D for me. ... Now I can buy my meds."

"The meds are a lot better now than they used to be. Before, they had me on ones that kept me depressed. Now I cycle between mild depression and just feeling normal. But still my brain isn't as sharp as it used to be. It may just be old age. I'm 56," he said, laughing.

"The meds keep me from hearing voices and seeing visions. I still hear voices once in a while in my head and see visions, but it's not like I did before. ... My therapist keeps an eye on me. He gets to see if I'm doing OK, able to pay my bills and not having another episode of mania. I see him once a week."

"It's sleeping that's nerve-wracking [when you're homeless]," he said. "You can get a camping or else a trespassing ticket if you're on private property. You have to pay 100 dollars or more than that for trespassing, and if you can't pay, you have to go to jail for a few days. But you've got to sleep somewhere.

"You have to get up at the crack of dawn and pack all your stuff up, so you can get out before someone sees you and calls the cops. Then you have to wait until dark to sneak back in. I had a pretty good place last year to be homeless, to camp out. It was in a park, but somebody found it out and stole my guitar," he said.

"Since I've been back I've been in jail about three times because I go manic when I'm not on my meds, and I get into trouble with the cops. I just talk with people sometimes and get too aggressive. I'm a Christian, and I'll tell people about my beliefs and stuff. They call the cops. ... I'm disrespecting the law.

"But I've never been in prison. I almost went once when I stole a car that I thought God gave me." He chuckled, looking a bit like Santa with his full white beard.

"I've been in mental institutions a lot more than [jail]. I've been in Fort Logan one time for a month and another time for three months, and I've been in two or three other times, to local mental places here in Boulder. ... Now I've settled down. ... I need to stick to my meds.

"I don't have a telephone. It's too expensive. I have a computer, but I'm not on the Internet. I just play games on it. I got another guitar, so I practice that a little bit. I'm not very good at it, but I like writing little songs, playing it. ... I don't have a TV. I listen to the radio."

Asked what keeps him going through the tough times, he said, "Faith in God that my life makes sense somehow. He takes care of me. Of course, I've been in trouble a lot because of my behavior. I don't blame myself because when you have a mental illness you're not your normal self. ... It's something different. If I go manic for too long, I go into a state of insanity where I have crazy ideas.

"Most important to me is my religion. If I can help other people, I do. I can't really help much with money, but talking about things. It's kind of hard for me because I've always been pretty much a shy person, kind of introverted, you know. But I'm trying to be more outgoing and friendly. I'll try to initiate conversations."

"I'm fine now. I pay rent, utilities, for my meds, psychiatrist, therapist, bus pass and food. Right now I'm saving to pay the $90 [annual] property tax on land I own in Arkansas. It's an acre in the country. ...I can't get food stamps or Medicaid because they want you to sell your land and I don't want to do that. I'll probably never have the money, but someday I hope to put a house or trailer on it. ... But I like Boulder a lot. I might just stick around here."

> It crashed around him when his first fierce bout of mental illness forced him to drop out of college and return home. This began a lifelong challenge to find mental and physical stability.

Jesse

Jesse

by Sharon Monroe

Early in his life, Jesse knew two things. He knew he was much more sensitive than others around him and he knew that he was called to the mountains. He was born in Inglewood, California. Unfortunately, he wasn't accepted at home for the ways he was different, spiritually sensitive, he said. He figured out, even as a kid, that in the Christian-based religion he was introduced to at home there was oppression of people who were seen as different, and oppression of women. School was hard for him. He wasn't accepted, and his spiritual gifts caused problems with those who didn't understand. He found himself retreating from contact with others. He decided at a young age that he wanted no part of various societal evils. He was overwhelmed by television news of violence, war and seeing others struggle to fit into society or overcome debt. He wanted something different, he said.

He was searching, searching. He tried drugs and alcohol; he tried living at Venice Beach, which he really loved. He tried college and he tried relationships. But none of those filled his need. When things went sour, he found himself sleeping in his truck for the first time on a cold night in February 2001, waiting for a warm meal outside a feeding center in Anaheim, California. BAM! A woman slammed into his truck. He learned that night that people take advantage of you when you're hungry and all you can think of is that warm meal across the street.

You're hungry, so you don't call the cops, even though it was certainly her fault, and you don't get all the information you need to access insurance. You're hungry, and that puts you at risk. Coping with something as important as feeding one's hunger makes it hard to navigate a crisis.

There were years of living in RVs, working part-time jobs, as many as three at a time, and still not getting enough money to move on. There were times of helping others and moving to Arizona to be there for a loved one.

> Coping with something as important as feeding one's hunger makes it hard to navigate a crisis.

Through it all Jesse started to sense a call, a leaning to the psychic/metaphysical world. By coincidence he heard about a famous medium in town for one night. Tickets were expensive, but Jesse knew he had to be there. The reading he heard confirmed that Jesse had psychic gifts and would do well to explore them, he said. Jesse began to practice and learned the rich aspects of his sensitivities; he was finally starting to understand. He realized that the shaman traditions he was exploring gave him guidance, insight and a path. He studied with metaphysical teachers and ministers in California. After years of searching, Jesse had found his people.

Jesse still wanted to come to the mountains.

As he tried once again, while driving toward the mountains his car overheated. He pulled off the highway into the breakdown lane, only to have a big rig hit him, he said. It was another setback to his move to the mountains, another random accident that deeply impacted his plan. It was so similar to that first night in his truck years before, outside the feeding center.

Eventually his metaphysical world brought him to Denver, then to Boulder. He currently has a van and a night-shift job, and he helps the non-housed in Boulder with his psychic skills and healing shamanic traditions. He helps those who need clarification, or just some guidance, in connecting who they are with others. He has found a way to encourage them. Good people have helped him when he needed it, he said. Every time he looks at the Flatirons he feels that Chief Niwot, among others, guided him here and continues to guide him.

His deceased maternal grandmother encourages and guides him, too.

Jesse wore a fedora with a white and gray feather in the hatband, a Hawaiian shirt and tan pants. He has a way of being open to those who come to talk to him. He welcomed friends who walked up with broad smiles.

He looks forward to his dream, to a future of living with others in a supportive community, close to the land, where they can learn from spiritual instructors and be self-sustainable.

He spoke of the nomadic life that some people choose because it fits them better. Sometimes housing doesn't work out because the people are happier in a nomadic lifestyle, he said. He is happy to share what he has learned with others who are open to it.

What three words would Jesse like to leave with us? He spread his arms and turned his palms to the sky. He smiled and almost sang, "I AM FREE!"

Mike

Mike

by Tim Johnson

Mike has done many things during his life, but when asked to give a brief sketch of himself, the first thing he said was, "I'm a father of two."

At no point does he mention that not long ago, he was rising in the ranks of a local marketing firm and earning a six-figure salary. There's no mention of his insatiable love for and extensive knowledge of music, his ability to set up a laptop without any software from Microsoft or Apple, or the fact that in 2003 he had some well-developed ideas about creating a social portal for college students, just prior to the emergence of the company that currently dominates that space. Instead, the single strongest piece of identity Mike clings to is being a father of two children: this clearly brings him the most joy, and also the most visible pain.

This writer has known Mike since 2003, when we met while working on a project together; I can personally vouch for the portal idea, and still kick myself for not listening to him. Mike was working in an infant online marketing industry and rising quickly. His mind seemed to work like a virtual idea factory, and I expected his career would rapidly outpace my own.

Now I was helping him pack up personal belongings as he left the house of one friend and headed to the house of another for a few days. When there are no vacancies at friends' houses, he sleeps in his car, or tries to find a safe place to camp if the weather is warm enough.

"Time for the big bag", Mike said with a smile, lifting a plastic bag containing at least 12 different medications. "This is less than last week!" he said, laughing. "The new doctor has really streamlined things." No matter how successful, no one is prepared for the sudden revelation of a major medical problem, and Mike didn't see it coming.

A few years ago Mike was laid off unexpectedly from a promising position with a local Denver company. Feeling resourceful and not expecting to be down for long, he never bothered to file for a COBRA insurance extension. A few months later he began to experience strange bouts of dizziness, sometimes enough to impair driving or even walking. Within a week he was diagnosed with multiple sclerosis, for which there is currently no cure. Without a job or insurance, his likely future played out quickly in his mind. He became emotionally devastated, and fell into a deep depression.

He lived with family and later with friends, while his outlook and prospects diminished until one day

> The homeless community themselves are just a good band of people. I was stunned.

there was literally no resource left from any direction. The economy had been hard on everyone. There was nothing left but the street.

"Once you're homeless, you're stigmatized," Mike said. "People stop listening, and start judging." Some friends have helped a great deal, he said, but others have fallen away entirely. Relationships with his family are strained at best. Asked to elaborate, he became quiet and said only, "We're no longer on speaking terms." After a pause he continued, "But there's one thing people need to remember, and it's that fathers love their children, no matter where they are or what their situation." I wondered about the last time he might have told them that himself, and how both sides felt during that conversation.

Asked what would surprise most people about being homeless, without hesitation he responded, "The people. Local service groups have been good, but the homeless community themselves are just a good band of people. I was stunned. I was probably somewhat bigoted before, but seeing it firsthand, it's completely different. People with nothing will offer you half of their sandwich or go out of their way to make sure you have a sleeping bag. There's no one-upmanship on the street; it's a real friendship at a fundamental level."

As in many cases, it was only after hitting bottom that Mike found access to medical treatment.

Unexpectedly, a doctor he had been seeing through local support groups determined the previous diagnosis of MS may be incorrect. His symptoms may be the result of a rare chronic inner ear disorder. He hopes to return to full-time work soon, and his dream remains to work in the music industry, leveraging his marketing skills to promote new talent.

Packing the last box into his car, he said, "I don't want to be a burden on anyone. But right now, my main focus is to get a handle on my medical condition so I can return to being a prosperous member of society."

On this sunny day, he seemed strong, sharp and capable of resuming his former life, able to be hired for or take on anything. The trunk closed, and we shook hands. "Thanks, buddy," he said, smiling broadly.

He pulled out and drove away, hoping for another chance further down the road.

Ronald

by Constance E. Boyle

For 33 years, beginning at age 14, Ronald was a land-scaper in Boulder; he was born here in 1959, and has lived here much of his life. In 1990 he received an associate's degree in design from a technology school in Westminster and during the 1990s he ran a company of 85 people. He designed and created more than 200 interior and exterior waterfalls in Boulder and the surrounding communities, many of which generated electricity to power homes. Ronald referred to his art form as "serene and surreal."

An accident while he was pulling a tree off a truck collapsed his spine in 1996. He sold his company, but continued to design and draft. Since then he has worked as a commercial landscaper and drafter in other loca-tions and soon will work full-time for Boulder Outreach for Homeless Overflow. His investments in Enron resulted in a tremendous financial loss for him, he said.

In the last 12 years, Ron has been homeless four times, this last time for about a year. He struggles with deep vein thromboses, or clots, on a daily basis. Because of congenital disabilities his veins are small and prone to clots. He also has a large hole in his heart that he said cannot be repaired because of anatomical chest cage problems.

Clinica Family Health Services in Boulder provides his ongoing medical care. He is currently on an anti-coagulant and the level has to be monitored. He said it is difficult to keep the level even, which is important in order to avoid side effects. Recently he passed out while in Denver waiting for a bus to keep a medical appointment. Not becoming discouraged, he expressed appreciation to strangers who helped him get to a hos-pital. His present benefits do not cover the monthly 190 dollars needed for a medication to help dilate his blood vessels and minimize clot formation. There is a lengthy waiting period for financial eligibility; it will be a relief when he can start the medication.

Clots became an issue after Ronald slipped on black ice on his way to work in 2010; he fractured his leg in several places and a large clot formed in his leg two weeks later. He is more restricted physically than he was prior to his injury because clots could become dislodged and travel to his heart, he said. He can't even ride a bike. In the past 18 months, he has had four surgeries requiring hospitalization and 14 "drainages" at Boulder Community Hospital. Asked how he maintains a positive attitude, he said, "I don't

> "When we say 'hi' to you on the street and you turn away and don't say a word, we're not invisible. Sometimes people just need some help."

Ronald

Ronald

let it get to me."

A frustrating thing about being on the street is that at night he has to keep moving all the time, under a blanket, to avoid the charge of "camping." He said he has become skilled at finding different places to sleep.

Ronald believes that being on the streets is dangerous for many people. He has helped some street people learn about available resources. "United we stand, divided we fall," is a favorite motto of his, he said, and he envisions a line of people in Boulder holding placards bearing those words. He wants to say to the non-homeless, "When we say 'hi' to you on the street and you turn away and don't say a word, we're not invisible. Sometimes people just need some help."

A few months ago Ronald said he helped reunite a 16-year-old from Houston, Texas, with his father. After finding the boy crying on the street and listening to his concerns, he called the father and told him the boy was frightened to return home. Because Ronald helped work things out, the outcome was positive. A few months later the boy called Ronald and asked how he could repay him. "Just pass it forward," Ronald said.

Despite his ongoing health issues Ronald remains very involved with the street people and their needs. In August 2011 he declared his candidacy for Boulder City Council, to help the homeless get off the streets, gain equal rights and make Boulder "the town it was 10 years ago." He said he remembers that Boulder had a nice charm and he pictures it in his mind with many more flowers.

He is writing a book about his experiences with blood clots. When his health is improved and the clots have resolved, he would like to fly-fish at Grand Lake again. He used to stand out on the rocks with waders, but would be happy to sit on a bank. Ronald also thinks of living in the United Kingdom; he has roots there. He is proud that his lineage goes back to Henry III.

As for his worldview, he quoted from a documentary about our planet: "It's not our planet. We're just using it."

Editor's Note: *On Sept. 14, 2011, Ronald announced the end of his campaign to be elected to Boulder City Council. His deep-vein thrombosis had worsened and he expected his leg might have to be amputated. He said he intended to devote his time to recovery from surgery and felt it would not be appropriate to run for office at that time.*

Leo

by Hollis Brooks

In the world of the homeless, 62-year-old Leo is considered a success story. After six years of sporadically living on the streets of Denver and Boulder, he now calls a comfy, secure, subsidized Walnut Place apartment "home". Adding to the good fortune of a stable living environment, he enjoys occasional work as a landscaper, under the supervision of folks he respects and even likes.

Leo, soft-spoken and mild in manner, was born in Putnam, Connecticut, to a family he described as "difficult, with many problems, including a dad with alcoholism who traveled constantly." His growing- up years were challenging, with cross-country moves to Seattle, then Palm Beach County, Florida, and finally Denver. Upon completing ninth grade, Leo worked odd jobs until he joined the military and went to Vietnam. After his Vietnam experience, he followed his father's path and joined the Merchant Marine as a deckhand. Life on a big ship provided Leo with an expanded vision of the world, and he reflected that "those years that combined steady hard work with travel were pretty happy for me."

As with many homeless, Leo's life on the street was the result of a sudden job loss. A longstanding telephone marketing job in Denver ended in 2004, and

> As with many homeless, Leo's life on the street was the result of a sudden job loss.

that, combined with what he described as "some bad investment decisions and a string of poor luck," led to being homeless on and off since then.

Asked what was toughest about living without a home, he said, "Three major things: keeping clean, having a secure place to sleep every night, and enduring bad weather."

Thanks to assistance from the social services system, steady support from the Carriage House Community Table, and the counsel and friendship provided by one very special advocate, Leo is now situated in his home. He credited Mary Katherine Jones, a case manager at Health Care for the Homeless, with helping him to get healthy and get established at Walnut Place.

As for money, "Living on 700 dollars in Social Security income isn't that hard," he said. "I don't need much." He pays 200 dollars toward monthly rent at Walnut Place and food is his only other major expense, so he eats some of his meals at the Carriage House Community Table.

Leo said he especially appreciates the small apartment at Walnut Place for the privacy it affords. It is his nest, where he can read about Scientology, practice Tae Kwon Do and research naturopathic health remedies for himself and his friends. "Krill oil, barley greens and

Leo

meditation have kept me pretty healthy for years," he said, although he does indulge in an occasional hand-rolled cigarette. For relaxation, Leo likes fishing and riding his bike.

In return for the help he has received, Leo demonstrates his gratitude. "He is caring and concerned about all of us," said Joy Eckstine, executive director of the Carriage House Community Table. "He sends me e-mail regularly, wondering how my health is and making sure to tell me all about his new findings in natural remedies. He is a gentle soul."

Asked to give advice to anyone facing homelessness, Leo counseled, "Tap into the services around you, really use them and keep in steady contact with the folks who run the organizations that help people in need of housing and health services.

"For me, assistance came from the Boulder Shelter [for the Homeless], Boulder Housing Partners, The Inn Between in Longmont, Senior Support Services and social services. And I still go to the Carriage House Community Table for meals and to talk with friends there. Just by being there I can show other folks going through rough times that the homeless life doesn't have to be a dead end." Most important, he continued, "Don't think that you can't or won't make your life better. Don't ever give up on yourself."

Dizzy Wind

by Marsha J. Perlman

"I'm in the middle of my gig on the Boulder Mall," were the first words Dizzy Wind said when I rang his cell phone to set a time for us to meet. The next afternoon, among shoppers, musicians, gawkers and vendors of hot dogs, pretzels and ice cream, we sat on a bench and talked about his current life in Boulder.

Asked how he got the name Dizzy Wind, he answered, "It's from a song I wrote."

With pride, the slim, neatly dressed man explained, "I'm homeless by choice, not by necessity." After many years as a chef in Estes Park, Colorado, he opted out of a traditional career and came to Boulder to live the life he enjoys.

He was explicit. "Outdoor living is in my blood and music is in my heart and soul. I'm here to camp, not live in the shelter. I love Boulder, especially the creek where I have my own little site along the water. It's not far from others who share my philosophy and social life."

Dizzy often plays his guitar more than eight to 12 hours a day. For him, his instrument, which he kept at his side while talking, has become so much a part of him that he doesn't want to do anything else. Along with several musicians he plans to record a CD this fall.

> "My culture buys few things, uses little fuel and other resources."

Dizzy shared his previous day. "I played and sang on the Mall in the afternoon and again in the evening and earned enough money to get whatever I had to get. Then spontaneously, I played music all night with another guitarist. Finally, this morning I helped a woman learn to play the mandolin. If you're sharing space with other people, you can't live like that."

Dizzy emphasized that his group of homeless people are not alcoholics or druggies, "but one big family that does a good job taking care of each other. We refer to ourselves as The Tribe. Many are transients who, for a month or two, get to know each other very well, then move on and meet up in different places weeks or months later."

At 16, he began his rambling life. "I was expelled from school for poor attendance and smoking pot," he said. "I met people and we hitched around the country. When I was 19, I began a four-year stint in the Coast Guard. Then I was married and divorced. My family includes three adult children, brothers and sisters. We keep in touch on Facebook. If they all lived as The Tribe does, eventually we'd bump into each other."

Dizzy explained how he experiences Boulder's attitude toward the homeless. "Most people here don't want to notice anyone who is homeless, whether it's by choice or circumstance. They assume we're all dirty and they don't want to see dirt." He added that people in The Tribe take showers several times a week.

He believes that anti-consumerism and anti-corporation are the major bonds among the homeless. He admits to having given up on the "weird lifestyle in America," and forecast the collapse of the financial system within 10 years.

"We're losing all our clean water and also people are living in large houses and being excellent consumers to keep the economy going, but that won't last. My culture buys few things, uses little fuel and other resources." He said he gets around Boulder by walking.

"If you look carefully, you'll notice that homeless people pick up litter to find effects for reuse or trade. We protect and enjoy the earth," he said. "For me, wading in the water is like a healing power."

He was emphatic that he doesn't care if the individuals he sees in Boulder know anything about him.

"I'd really like it if they just forgot about me and I slowly disappeared into the mountains," he said.

When reminded that those people's tips support him, he responded, "I make money doing what I *want* to do, not what I *have* to do but dislike doing. If they think I'm good, and most seem to because I get a lot of attention, I'll accept their money."

Dizzy had plans to join friends who were waiting for him.

I returned the following evening to listen to him entertain on the west end of the Pearl Street Mall, where he maintains a good base of listeners from restaurants, bars and patios.

Barefoot, Dizzy fancy-stepped to the rhythms of the songs he sang and played. His supporters tapped their feet to the beat of his music, several sang or hummed, one couple danced and most of the audience dropped bills into his open guitar case.

"Rabbit"

"Rabbit"

by Jerrie Hurd

"We got the greatest homeless community in the world, man. Some homeless used to be professors, you know. Sure, we get some idiots from Denver, but the new bunch of shelter rats we got now are mostly right on," said Eric, 31, describing his fellow homeless with family pride.

Rabbit, the name he prefers, is described by the staff at the Carriage House Community Table as "one of the good guys." When new people show up, especially kids, he looks out for them. "Yeah, I guess I'm good at talking to people," he said. "First time out here, it's rough, and sometimes you just have to say, hey, it's not that bad, and I show them where there's food and stuff — no reason to be hungry in Boulder. Anybody can be real grumpy when you're hungry, you know, so I show everybody around and make sure they stay out of trouble."

He should know. He was 17 years old when he first hit the street. He has been taking care of himself and his community for 12½ years — long enough that he has no tolerance for those who do hard drugs, rip off others or exhibit predatory behaviors. "We got a nice, tight-knit community here, and we keep track of who's doing what, and who's stealing what, and we take care of all that stuff ourselves. We don't call the cops or nothing; we just take care of it, and the cops respect our decision, too."

Rabbit has a cell phone, a storage unit with his tools in it, a backpack and a bike. He can be seen riding around Boulder looking for work. He is skilled in the construction trades and can do roofing, painting, electrical. Most recently he has added security systems to the list. "I wasn't worried about reading the blueprints, but I wasn't so sure about the programming part until I realized it was in English, and, s___, I can do English."

As he talks, he points to various buildings where he says he has done the roof or moved the walls or put down the concrete underneath. Winters are always slow, but the combination of slow season and deep recession means he is particularly short of paid jobs. He thinks it would help if he could search wider. He tried to get a bus pass but that didn't pan out for him. Needing work, wanting work, is a constant theme. "I've got skills; I got pictures of the work I've done, man. I just need to be doing something."

The cross Rabbit wears around his neck was ordered on the Internet and delivered to the Carriage House Community Table. "We check the Internet; we know who's who and what's what and what's going on," he continued, adding that the cross is one of his favorite things because he likes glow-in-the-dark stuff in

> "I show everybody around and make sure they stay out of trouble."

general. In particular, he wears it to remind himself to stay out of trouble. That is especially important because he's getting close to the end of his probation and he has big plans.

In four months he wants to go to Mill Creek, Washington, and work with a martial arts master he admires. For the last three years` he has concentrated on learning various martial arts. Now he wants to work with the best so he can get certified. Then he can teach martial arts. This fits with his strong sense of community. He can't be everywhere, taking care of everyone, so he wants to teach people how to take care of themselves. "It's a mean, bad world," he said, "but women, even small little girls, can defend themselves." He believes that is possible because he knows that martial arts work, no matter how big the bad guy is.

Last summer his admired master offered Rabbit a place in his school but his probation officer wouldn't let him go out of state. He has had several probation officers since then and none will allow him to leave the area, even though the staff at the Carriage House Community Table tried to help him. Frustration is audible in his voice. In four months he will be off probation, and then he'll be gone. He gets noticeably excited when he talks about his plans and about martial arts he has tried — the latest is a meditative form of archery.

Rabbit's upbeat attitude is noticeable. "Life is attitude, man. They can take everything from me but my attitude. I get to decide that, don't I?" On the other hand, he said he hates the attitude he gets from people who see him around Boulder. He describes it as dumb-prejudice and wishes people would just wish him a good day or something. "Tell me to keep my head up," he said. "Who doesn't need that?"

Eddie

Eddie

by Curtine Metcalf

> To Eddie, the non-judgmental homeless community offers far greater comfort ... than the biological family he hails from.

Eddie is both unconventional and typical. He characterized his upbringing in the eastern and southern parts of the United States as having "a good childhood in a hard- core Christian home," where he had "no room to explore other religions." In a family atmosphere he called "tense about religion," he said he was "belted" when he did not embrace the same religious beliefs. When Eddie was 15, he, his parents and three siblings moved to Colorado.

Eddie talked about his earlier, "darker days" of tinkering in an unhealthy life that faded into alcohol and drugs. This took him on a path to explore his own religion. He discovered a "theistic" religion that his "family fully disagrees with." Still, he is in touch with his family every two weeks or so.

Now in his late 30s, Eddie became homeless more recently, when he was evicted from the home he rented and luckily found a bed at the Boulder Shelter for the Homeless. On cold nights when the shelter is full, he finds his way to warmth in the "overflow warming" spaces that a few churches and other facilities offer through Boulder Outreach for Homeless Overflow. Eddie and other homeless people are grateful for a warm place they can lay their heads. They also appreciate the food that is available through the Carriage House Community Table's 5 o'clock "feeds," and through churches, Community Food Share and local food banks that collect and redistribute food from grocery stores that would otherwise go to waste.

One challenge of being homeless relates to health issues. Eddie called his health problems "a ball and chain" from which he cannot escape. He said his health is one of the main things keeping him homeless. His cell phone offers him a way to "stay in touch with the times" as he works his way through the system, getting what he is able to and qualified for, through Medicare and other programs. He hopes for a new home with the help of a housing voucher through Boulder County's Shelter Plus Care Program.

Eddie wants and desperately needs the camaraderie and "family" that the Boulder homeless community provides and that supports him daily. To Eddie, the non-judgmental homeless community offers far greater comfort mentally, emotionally and spiritually than the biological family he hails from. Eddie has chosen to be "homeless" for now. He has adopted children and still longs for love, a good job and a healthy marriage and family. Eddie said he does "not believe in hope or prayer – just life," his own god and the fact that he makes his own choices.

Gregory

by Mary Beth Lagerborg

Gregory stood under a shade tree in a parking lot on a muggy July day in intermittent rain. His yellow Lab rested peacefully on his side under the tree. Greg will not step far from his dog, which he's named Dog, but pronounces "dee-oh-gee."

Greg is from Detroit, and he purchased Dog when he was three weeks old as a birthday present for his wife. When he and his wife divorced soon afterward, Greg said he got the better end of the deal. She got the house and the car; he got Dog.

The two of them hit the road. Greg had been a hard drinker, but gave it up to look after Dog. He was homeless, but he wasn't looking for trouble. "Dog is my kid," said Greg. "I tell people, 'Dog rescued me,' and he did. I love him very much. He's always been by my side."

But he nearly lost his friend. At a campsite near Tallahassee, a man sicced his pit bull on Dog, and it tore off his hind leg. People advised Greg to put down Dog by the side of the highway, but by the grace of God, Greg said he found Northwood Animal Hospital.

When he wasn't given any hope there, Greg put all $1,400 that he had on the table and said, "Well, just keep him alive until tomorrow."

The receptionist called in the vet, who asked everyone else to leave the room and said, "You go sit down, put your money back in your pocket, and give me Dog." They kept Dog for a month, performing the necessary surgeries and nursing him back to health.

While Dog recovered and was physically rehabilitated, Greg stayed at The Shelter in Tallahassee. Although animals normally aren't allowed at shelters, they took in Greg and Dog.

Once the dog was well they resumed their journey, walking from Florida to Boulder. "I never intended to get this far, but the state lines just kept coming up: Welcome to Alabama, Welcome to Louisiana, Welcome to Mississippi."

Greg said he is thankful for the kindnesses shown to him and Dog. But his greatest day-to-day trials are with folks who seem to assume that because he's homeless, he must be mistreating the dog.

"Like yesterday, I bought flax seed at Alfalfa's," he said. "I put flax seed in his food. I know what he likes. But here's a woman right away, 'Hey, that dog needs some water.'

"Well, there was clearly a bowl of water right in front of him; and in fact, it was cold water. And I said, 'Ma'am, don't you see the water right there?' And she just acted

> His greatest day-to-day trials are with folks who seem to assume that because he's homeless, he must be mistreating the dog.

Gregory

by Mary Beth Lagerborg

like she didn't hear me. And so she kept up with it. So I'm a pretty good guy, and I don't say nothing to too many people, because I'm in a spot and you don't want any hassles. But after you get told about your dog 20 times a day, every day, finally I said, 'Look, lady, I'm sick of you people telling me how to take care of my dog. He's probably the best-looking dog in Boulder.'"

Dog has kept them homeless longer than they might have been. It's difficult to find a job to which Greg can bring him. "And I'm not going to leave him with nobody," he said, "especially a homeless person."

Greg now has a job, the result of another kindness. ARES Thrift Store in Boulder provides dress clothes for homeless people going to job interviews. Greg was there to get outfitted, and afterward the owner chased him down to ask, "Why don't you come work for me?"

"Well, I do have Dog," he said.

"Well, bring Dog to work with you," she said.

"It was a big opportunity for me. Not a whole lot of money, you know, but to a homeless person that has nothing, it is a great deal. … I was very lucky. I think jobs are the answer, just like any politician would tell you," Greg said. "Jobs are the answer for the people who do want to work. Sometimes they don't even have that choice because there is no jobs. They are just thrown in with the rest of the homeless population, even though their problems may be different. They are put together with everybody with a label put on you: you're homeless, you're crazy, you've got a backpack. Run the other way. This one has a dog. Run faster, Spot, run faster, Dog is a killer.

"So that's the way it is. I have to go to work. I can't be late for this job," said Greg, and gathered Dog's food bowl and water, so they could walk down the street.

Bryan

Bryan
by Cheri Hoffer

"I'm just basically a happy person," said Bryan. Sustained by song lyrics, Bryan said, "I wake up singing and I go to bed singing," He wakes up under bridges and in tents that have to be moved every day, even during bitter winters and mosquito-ravaged summers. We talked on the street in February because he said local business owners won't let him through their doors. Bryan quietly established himself as an intelligent, remarkably resourceful man. "I'm a finder … I find money, clothes, even electronics…. I am not a thief."

Well-groomed and articulate, Bryan doesn't present like any stereotype of the homeless. At 42, he is introverted by nature, insisting that he is able to get through our interview only because Joy at the Carriage House Community Table requested it. There, he and others can shower, enjoy hot meals on weekdays, access the Internet, medical and mental health services and get employment counseling.

Clearly, Bryan could teach a class of his own on street smarts, starting with finding street lamps that have power outlets to charge a cell phone and iPod, and heat water to keep his friends in coffee. The interior world he creates while listening to his music is a calm and welcoming one, unlike the social and physical world around him.

> Bryan is bucking the odds, 14 months sober and counting.

Bryan, an alcoholic only child raised by an alcoholic only child was displaced, beaten and eventually molested by one of a string of boyfriends and father figures. His birth father walked out when he was six months old. His mother's father walked out when she was six years old. The intergenerational patterns are unmistakable. Yet Bryan is bucking the odds, 14 months sober and counting. He said he "prays hard" for a future in which, "Number one, I want to remember my life. My time is short." A future of sobriety means a major rift between himself and his girlfriend of seven years, who has been unable to give up drinking.

Having survived life on the streets through cancer, asthma, alcoholism, panic disorder and months of jail time, Bryan has a strength that will serve him in sobriety. Telling his story with no self-pity, he brightened and added, "It's not all depressing." He shares hard-won wisdom with great patience: In the depths of winter put a bottle of hot water in the foot of your sleeping bag to avoid frostbitten toes; keep secret storage places to stash sleeping bags and tarps for others; know who is serving food, where and when.

Long ago Bryan earned $28 an hour as a forklift driver, but an industrial accident left him with a bad back and no job. Drinking to ease pain was familiar. "It's a really bad cycle," he said. "You wake up sick with a headache and body aches. You drink again to feel better. It takes 15 minutes to feel better. You get drunk, go to bed and wake up sick.

"I've been to the ARC [Alcohol Recovery Center] 97 times … the place for drunks and stupid people." Hitting bottom in 2010, Bryan stole a bicycle in an alcoholic blackout and wound up in jail for 63 days. With time on his hands he studied a booklet that he credits with saving his life, Easy Way to Quit, by Alan Carr. "It tells the complete truth about how evil alcohol really is," he said, destroying lives in "a trick of lights." Primed for change, he quit tobacco and alcohol and is now facing the demons that have plagued him all his life. "I'm socially underdeveloped and diagnosed with panic disorder. I don't know if I can get back into society. If the bus gets too crowded I get clammy, see black spots and pass out." Medications had unacceptable side effects. Yet Bryan is pushing on.

He counts about 25 members in his trusted tribe of homeless family. "When one of ours is dying we try to get in touch with their kids. In Boulder County 26 homeless people died in 2010. The last one froze to death at 28 years old."

There is some loss when one among them manages to secure housing. "When somebody gets a place of their own they are not coming back soon. They get a place and try to come back later and it doesn't work. They're starting another life. I get invited but I don't feel good enough to go."

Success for Bryan means having an address where he can receive mail, get ID and be able to vote. "It means having a place where my two girls can find me. And I want to be an asset to society where I can help my community." This dream is straight from the heart. "Years ago I made promises to my mother that I would get her a house." Bryan's mother was living on the street when she died from alcoholism and emphysema in 2008. Bryan wants a different life and seems determined to get it.

Jerry

by Craig Yager

"Hello? I just missed the bus. I'll be late." It was Jerry calling. Polite and concerned, he didn't want me to think he wasn't coming to our appointment. "I can get there around 11:30. Will that be all right?" He didn't want to waste my time waiting for him, wondering.

I first saw Jerry several years ago at the Saturday morning Farmers' Market in Boulder. I ignored him, walking past without a smile or a nod or any recognition that he was there. Neglect didn't seem to faze this man. Regardless of how many people did the same, he still smiled and approached the next person in the crowd with enthusiasm and pride in the product he sells – The VOICE.

Jerry was Boulder's first vendor of The Denver VOICE, a newspaper dedicated to telling the stories of the homeless and offering them an economic incentive. Jerry was one of the original six vendors when the first issue came out. Now there are close to 1,000 people who, like Jerry, pay a quarter for each copy, asking customers for a dollar donation, and get to keep 75 cents per paper sold. In the early days of this newspaper, there wasn't a distribution source for Boulder. Jerry saw a market and took initiative. Riding the bus down to Denver each week, he returned, arms full, smiling. His livelihood took root.

Jerry invests much of his earnings in the people he loves. He often travels to Oklahoma to visit his twin brother. He checks in with relatives along the East Coast, being originally from Queens, New York. Occasionally, he sees friends in California. His face lights up most when he talks about trips to New Hampshire. "The trees there are beautiful in October," he said. Traveling by Greyhound and Amtrak, Jerry connects with people around the country, but said, "Boulder is my home for now." When he's in town, he stays with friends or at the homeless shelter. He said he thinks about moving to live with his brother, but the beauty of Boulder's mountains and the job he enjoys so much keep him here. "The scenery, the historical buildings and the nice parks, like Chautauqua, are beautiful. Very beautiful."

Jerry embodies the spirit of Boulder in his hopes and dreams. "I'd like to go back to school and learn about climate and be able to do something to help the environment." He paused. "But, when I really think about it, I like what I'm doing. I really like selling the paper. It's a good thing. I'm my own boss. I can choose my hours. I'm the one in charge."

He would like the people of Boulder to know how dedicated he is. "I'm kind-hearted and a hard worker and I get things accomplished." When he's not working, he likes to read and he likes to walk. "Walking is good."

> "I'm kind-hearted and a hard worker and I get things accomplished."

Does he have worries? Like any businessman, he fends off worry with deliberate optimism. "If you do what's right, everything usually turns out pretty good. Yeah, pretty good. It doesn't pay to worry."

Fiercely independent, full of ownership in what he does, Jerry also enjoys meeting people while working. Many don't give him the time of day, but still he tries to see the best in everyone. Gretchen Crowe, director of the vendor program at The Denver VOICE, said, "Jerry is my inspiration. He exemplifies the best of what this newspaper is designed to do by optimizing what we offer in every way possible. It makes me happy to see him thrive."

Jerry impresses most people who take time to talk with him. Interviewing Jerry in the Daily Camera in May 2010, staff writer Laura Snider described him as "unflappably kind and courteous to customers." As Jerry sells papers, the description fits him perfectly. Even when people aren't nice to him, Jerry said, "I try to be nice to them."

During the winter, when the Farmers' Market is closed, Jerry is often seen on the northwest corner of Pearl and Broadway, where we were to meet for this interview. As in all his contacts with people, he cared enough to track down a phone, make an apologetic call and let us know he had missed the bus and was going to be late. Being someone who knows that time is money, he didn't want to waste ours. That's the kind of person Jerry is.

Steve T.

by Ann Brandt

"I'm technically not homeless," Steve said as we met. He explained that he had a room at the Carriage House Community Table in Boulder, as facility manager of the organization. He had, however, been homeless on and off for 11 years. Leaving Alaska in 1991, he had traveled to Seattle and then "backpacked around the country" with his guitar.

Music is Steve's passion. His own music style was influenced by singers of the 1960s and 1970s, and he is proud to say that he has attended eight Arlo Guthrie performances. He said one of his dreams is to one day find some way to provide instruments for homeless musicians and form a band, incorporating storytelling into the music. A lot of stories can be shared with music, he said. He mused about how this storytelling with music could be incorporated into a job skills training process.

Steve has stories to tell about his adventures and the unique method he used to give up drinking alcohol. He had been sharing a trailer with a friend, pretty much doing nothing more than drinking beer and smoking pot. After attending an AA meeting he poured a great amount of beer down the sink. The pot, he admitted, took a little longer to get rid of. But he has been clean and sober for over three years, never looking back. He had no trouble, he said,

in giving up drugs and alcohol once he made the decision. It was simply "a miracle," he said.

Spirituality and faith in God threads through Steve's philosophy on life in general. He would like to talk more about his faith in Jesus but said he feels that today's political correctness discourages talking about God and Jesus in public places — another facet of society that shows our indifference to each other as individual human beings through adherence to rules.

Spirituality and faith in God threads through Steve's philosophy on life in general.

Steve said there is a lack of caring in our society and that we need to care for and about each other. We need to slow down and take the time to look at and listen to other people and what they are really saying and feeling. Too much emphasis is on what we have and who we think we are and not enough on how we act toward each other. When we ask someone how they are, for example, we are not generally asking for details; the question is merely a formality.

Steve said he would like to see the "stigma against homeless people" erased. Homeless people are not usually involved in violent crime, he said; most of their crime is perpetrated "by homeless on homeless." While there is no typical homeless person, Steve said the people who stand on street corners begging are "broken people." He sees alienation in today's society that causes him to believe the world is "broken." He wants us to climb out of our artificial lives, look at and listen to each other.

Steve has developed coping skills for all situations. "I can work both sides —present myself well." He spoke of maintaining a neat, well-kept appearance and using good manners in all situations, especially when hitchhiking. "I try to be the best person I can be and encourage others to be their best." Three times as we spoke, someone walked in and out of the room, needing various answers that only he could provide. He remained unruffled by the interruptions.

Asked about his weaknesses, he voiced his disdain for paperwork. Then, when asked what he wishes he could have done differently, Steve didn't hesitate. Although he is at peace with himself now, he said he wishes he had gotten rid of anger sooner. "But that's

what I saw at home."

He said that while his stepfather did not physically abuse him, there was always a threat: "The fist in the face," he said, was especially scary for a little kid because you never knew what was coming next. He now believes that harboring anger against those who have hurt us is not helpful in maintaining a healthy outlook, and he demonstrated that with his next thought. "You have to look at what they [my parents] knew," he said, explaining their lack of parenting skills. In understanding their situation he has forgiven them by getting rid of past anger, and that, he said, is what the Bible tells us to do.

How long does he think he will stay in one spot? There is no definite time. Right now he has a job and a place to stay.

Michael F.

Michael F.

by Jodi Burnett

Gentleness, compassion and a positive outlook radiate from Michael, a 59-year-old homeless man who lives in Boulder. Although he was born and raised in the small town of Menomonee Falls, Wisconsin, near Milwaukee, Michael is now as much of a Boulderite as any true native. He loves the city, its people and especially its mountains and creek. Boulder has been his home for 32 years. "If you love where you're at, it doesn't matter if you sleep in a creek bed or a mansion," he said of his adopted city. Growing up in a Catholic home in the Midwest, Michael was the middle child of five siblings. After high school he left home to see the world. Choosing not to go to college immediately following high school was a determining factor in his life. It is the one thing he said he would do differently if he could do it all over again.

Michael has held jobs but he tended to get restless, quit and end up homeless again. Michael was struggling with addiction and lack of commitment, both of which made it difficult to stay with one job for long. He has gained extensive experience, a pension and a 401(k) through various jobs but it was while working for CU's Special Event Security at a college graduation that Michael was inspired to achieve his own degree.

> It was while working for CU's Special Event Security at a college graduation that Michael was inspired to achieve his own degree.

With the help of grant money, he managed to put himself through two years at Front Range Community College and then a final two years at Metropolitan State College, graduating in 2008 with a bachelor's degree in history. While he was in school he was able to use some of his funding to provide housing for himself, but after he graduated he faced homelessness once again.

Michael is proud of his integrity and sense of loyalty. His strong faith assures him that God is always there for him. He spends his time working for the Carriage House Community Table, reading, staying up-to-date on current events and utilizing the assistance of programs such as Deacon's Closet and the local emergency warming centers. Michael prefers to work rather than "flying a sign," which he feels is humiliating. He would like to have a job in customer service, but finds it difficult to get hired without a permanent residence.

Michael is effectively an ambassador for the homeless community in Boulder. His main goal is to get people off the streets and into programs for addiction, mental health and education. He believes it is important to help others, which he currently does through his work at the Carriage House Community Table, assisting with meal preparation for

other homeless people. Oddballs, an odd-jobs business, is another organization Michael works with, connecting homeless people with opportunities to earn money. He is also active in the movement to change the city's policy on ticketing homeless people for camping. He would like to see the city designate areas for the homeless to sleep outside in the summer. "Some people feel they own the whole city just because they live in a house."

Homelessness has forced Michael to face his past and his addictions. It has allowed him to really work on himself without distraction. Consequently, he is more grateful for everything: meals, sleeping inside and all the volunteers who are trying to help. Being homeless has also helped him become more people-conscious and he has learned not to judge others. "Get to know someone who is homeless before you judge," he advised. Michael fights against the stigma that comes with homelessness. "It is hard not to lose your personhood." From his perspective, the worst part of homelessness is seeing young people on the streets throwing their lives away. "They can't get a break and they don't give themselves a break either." Michael wishes that homeless people were not lumped all into one box. He would like the "house people" not to stereotype all homeless people as addicts and bums. "There are so many people out here who are educated, talented and creative. Everyone is worth the trouble," he said, adding, "You can't put the house people in a box either."

Michael would like to act as a liaison between the homeless community and the many organizations trying to help. He is intelligent, articulate and has a deep personal knowledge of the needs of the homeless. Both communities trust him. "The homeless need help but don't know how to ask for it," he said. Michael wants to assist in the process. He feels the worst thing would be to just give up. His positive attitude and compassion for others is infectious. He feels he has hope for others, hope they may not have for themselves. In one year, Michael will begin receiving his small retirement benefits. He hopes to be able to afford a home then. He believes his best years are still ahead of him.

Chris

by Carol Grever

Crossing the bridge to the Boulder Public Library, Chris is indistinguishable from the homeless people warming themselves among the bookshelves. Dark wool stocking cap pulled low over shoulder-length hair, his heavy boots and layered clothing defy frigid January winds outdoors. With his stubbly beard, he blends into the community of "his people."

At 43, Chris's eventful life might have crushed him, but his sincere brown eyes and kindly South Carolina accent soften hard realities of his past. This advocate and servant of the displaced people of Boulder shines with positive energy.

Growing up as a fundamentalist preacher's kid, he rebelled as a teenager, then married young. After his 13-year marriage ended in divorce, he felt uprooted. He had no plan, no direction, no idea where he'd go next. Then, he said, "God spoke to me."

"What are you going to use me for?" Questioning, he stumbled on a backpack, lost on the street. Inside was a map of the United States. That was his sign to travel —somewhere. He took that first step and didn't look back. During four years of homeless wanderings, Chris somehow felt *led*. "There is a purpose. Don't worry, have faith."

"I caught a ride in a semi from Cincinnati to Denver. Just had a blanket when I got here. Some kids took me up to Nederland and I ended up camping in the mountains. I blended in pretty good in Ned."

Camping was a time of healing for Chris, a yearlong spiritual journey. He quit his cocaine habit and got a job at a smokehouse/brewery in town. Sharing his camp with a girlfriend, the freshness of nature brought him physical and mental healing. He lived in the moment.

During this time, a pair of ravens "adopted" Chris. The birds seemed to follow him, even around town. As months passed, trouble brewed when his girlfriend started using drugs again. Conflicted, Chris looked for guidance and the ravens' role became clear. The male disappeared, gone for good. Chris had his sign and walked away in a March snowstorm. Well acquainted with the ways of the streets, he dealt weed in Boulder, slowly losing his way.

Depressed, malnourished, with no sense of guidance, Chris decided he'd strike out for Oregon. The night before he planned to leave, he went to the Homeless Shelter for one good night's sleep. Waiting there was an unexpected note from a man he'd met months before. The note offered a cabin in Wondervu, free of rent in return for fixing the place up. "I was rescued," Chris said, grinning.

> Chris somehow felt *led*. "There is a purpose. Don't worry, have faith."

Chris

Once again, he followed the path that opened before him. He reveled in vast mountain views and fresh nature. He worked on the cabin and got a paying job at a Mexican restaurant. "Still growing, still alone," except for his dog. Two years passed quietly in Wondervu, then another turning point came when Chris fell in love with a woman he met in Boulder. With a new sense of stability, he found an anchor and a mission. Boulder's homeless became his real community and he began to feel responsible for everyone on the street.

Pursuing his purpose, he adopted the homeless community and is respected as their comrade and leader. "I went legit," he said, and now serves as manager of operations at Boulder Outreach for Homeless Overflow, the coalition of faith congregations that provides warm shelter and food to homeless people on cold Colorado nights. He volunteers at the Carriage House Community Table, a daytime service center for homeless and mentally ill people, and he does street outreach for Attention Homes, befriending and rescuing homeless teens. He recruited street people for a community cleanup project and to donate earnings to a poor African village—giving back even though they have so little. His recent project is FEED: Friends Encouraging Eating Daily, a program to feed the needy on holidays and at times when other free food is not available. "At Central Park, the old weed table is now the FEED table!" he said.

Chris continues to follow the guidance he receives from his basic spiritual values. He still feels led, receiving what he needs. He senses purpose even when it isn't clearly seen. "My life is full of signs, but I'm still not sure this is the end of my mission." The homeless are his *family* but they are only one of several groups he hopes to bring together. He seeks connection and understanding among five communities: the homeless, private citizens, business, government and faith-based groups.

Chris and his lady have a place to live now, with her seven-year-old son and their brand-new baby. But his heart remains on the street with his people. "I'm just an everyday guy, maybe with some God-given gifts — kindness, work ethic, leadership. I get up every morning and try to change the world. At the end of my life, I hope I can say I used everything God gave me."

Scott

Scott

by Constance E. Boyle

For three months, Scott has been living in Boulder, in his van. It's become a way of life for him over the last few years. He has lived in Denver and Boulder for 20 years and spent the last two winters in Tempe, Arizona.

Scott was born in New York City in 1957; he moved with his family to Arizona at age five, where he stayed until 1970. He graduated from Chicago's Lane Technical High School in 1975, completed a half-year of college at Southern Illinois University, and then had a Pell Grant to study art at the Art Institute in Chicago where he took night classes.

Scott believes that he's both a typical and not-so-typical homeless person. He goes to soup kitchens and gets free clothes. He's particular about how he dresses and about staying clean; showering at the Carriage House Community Table, cleaning up in Laundromats ("I get there early") or utilizing the facilities at parks. He saves Handi Wipes from grocery stores, and says, "It's the easiest way to clean fast."

But instead of worrying about where to sleep or hang out at night, he worries about where it's legal to park and how long he can park in a particular place. "Wal-Mart parking lots are safest, you can stay overnight."

"Being homeless successfully has a certain responsibility," Scott said. In order to get jobs he needs to keep a clean record and can't use substances or sleep in the park. If he gets arrested, it looks bad.

Scott gets temp jobs and feels he's resourceful, although he admitted he's good at getting jobs and not so good at keeping them. He gets laid off frequently and said he doesn't completely understand why this is. He does know that he has difficulty handling stress and that as his stress level increases, after a few weeks his productivity goes down. Scott also believes that in this economy, more and more jobs are temporary, which he feels also explains why his jobs are short-term. He'd rather have a long-term job, but a temp job is a good alternative.

"If there's a way to make money and it's legal, I've thought about it," he said. Recently he had a medical supply assembly job for 5½ weeks and he will start a telephone sales job in the Boulder area soon, after he trains for the position. He can type 30 words per minute with 96 percent accuracy and likes jobs that involve computers, including cashier jobs. He has worked as a $10.50-per-hour bus driver. He also drove a shuttle but his class C license has expired. Scott said the larger the vehicle, the harder to maneuver, and he thinks he'd be sideswiping cars now if he drove a truck.

> "Being homeless successfully has a certain responsibility."

When in Arizona he donates plasma twice a week and is paid $240 per month. "Not everyone wants that spike in their veins," he said, "but I don't mind." He likes the fact that you have to have blood tests done to qualify as a donor, which gives him information about his health. He has no health problems.

Scott said he keeps coming back to "good and bad, culture and poverty." While he was somewhat cryptic, my perception was that he sees and experiences life as polarities.

He'd "like to be a luxury homeless person in an RV or live full-time in a trailer park, or get an inexpensive trailer in a senior park," he said.

He practices Buddhism, he explained, because Buddhism accepts homeless people, with a history of wandering monks for thousands of years. Scott believes a Buddhist perspective and living in a Buddhist way is helpful to him as he encounters life. His art to living: stay positive and have enough money.

Don

Don

by Curtine Metcalf

Meet "The High Plains Drifter," as he has been known for many years, named after the Clint Eastwood character in the movie of that name. It doesn't matter what his given name is any more. He has taken this persona and wears it well. He is proud, clear and positive, has an incredible memory for dates, places and events, and is totally on top of his finances. Yes, he has finances that he manages. He unquestionably states that he is free. Free from debt, free from obligation to anyone or anything, except a storage space, which he has already paid for through the fall, and free to be the adventurer that he loves being.

The High Plains Drifter, seldom referred to by his given name, Don, left his Illinois farm home in 1969 as the "black sheep." Smack dab in the middle of five kids, he and his father were "two very different people," he said. So he joined the Air Force at 19, got home from his induction and found a draft notice waiting for him. Luckily he had beaten the draft by joining that day and he spent the next three years in Thailand serving his country.

Although both parents are now gone, Don has continued to go home to help with the family farming. It's in his blood; he's been driving a tractor since he was 7. He was adamant that the family farmland north of Chicago be willed to his youngest brother after his parents died. "He deserves it. He was the one who took care of my parents throughout their aging process. He is the one who should have it." His brother eventually moved to Missouri to farm, where the Drifter now travels twice annually to visit and help him. April and September are the most weather-friendly months for traveling; he saves enough for a bus ticket and off he goes. He does not keep in touch with the rest of the family and they do not understand how he lives. This brother is his family and that's enough for him. He emphasized that in his travels cross-country he has never found or looked for trouble.

Don said he lives by the adage, "Treat others as you would like to be treated," and believes in live and let live. As a homeless person in Boulder he is often snarled at with, "Why don't you get a job?" He answers with, "Why don't you hire me?" The truth is, he does work here and there when he can find a job. He has worked with one of the regular vendors at the Boulder Creek Festival for about 10 years, hauling ice and trash, and doing what needs to be done. For that he gets some great meals and a little cash. He sees it as one of his working adventures in the survivalist life he has chosen. Prospecting for gold in Boulder Creek has also called his name and he has "cashed in some" at a local jewelry store.

The Drifter carries just about everything he needs on his person. Each pocket is reserved for specific items; in one is an old-fashioned knife sharpener, the Edgemaker Pro. Sharpening knives and scissors is a service he offers for a reasonable price, a real old-fashioned process that uses no oil and costs $5. He said that using WD-40 as many do "opens the pores of the steel and contaminates the food it comes in contact with." Another pocket is a mini-desk with writing utensils and papers and other desk-type things. There's a mini-food pocket and a cell phone pocket; the phone is used for very select and important contacts, all pre-paid minutes. He noted that his belongings constitute not too much, not too little, but just enough for his needs. His distinctively decorated feathered hat and heavy coats serve as his warmth, protection from the sun in the summer and cold in the winter. His umbrella is a shelter in the rain and a safe place to retreat to. They are all one – he, his hat and coats, like an outer skin.

Don has been homeless on and off since 1969. He first heard about Boulder in 1977, "just after they had finished planting the tree saplings on the Pearl Street Mall." He is one of the many who have come to this valley and never left. He said he doesn't get lonely by himself. "It's much easier to be able to just take care of yourself," he said, but he still has his camaraderie on the streets and the "sheltered" places they tuck into to rest; to bed at dark and up with the light.

The High Plains Drifter chooses to be without a house, not without a home. "Mother Earth is home," he said, "and if you want to do it, you can live without 'stuff.'"

> "Mother Earth is home," he said, "and if you want to do it, you can live without 'stuff.'"

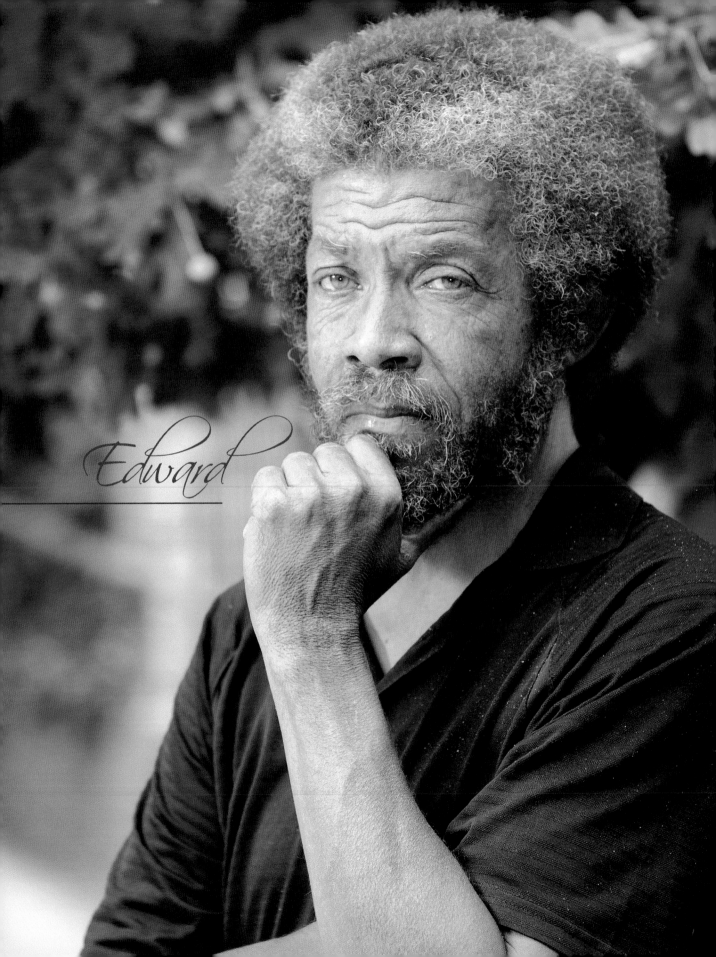

Edward

Edward

by Elle Page

Edward loves language. He was intrigued by my French name and knew its meaning. "Did you study French?" I asked. "I dabbled in it but I really focused on Latin." He then shared his passion for words: "I study etymology and semantics. I like to read so I often go to the library and read the dictionary. The shortened version of my name, 'Ed,' means witness and, of course, it's a common suffix denoting past tense."

Sound high-brow? Edward said he studied psychology at Yale, "not specifically for a career but it was an effective vehicle." He said he was there from 1969 to 1973; tumultuous years, but he didn't want to pursue that topic.

"I needed to go to another place so I came to the University of Denver for my teaching certificate and was a substitute teacher in Denver," he said. In 1985 he "wanted to take a year to wander." He's been wandering, homeless since then.

Ed's wandering is now local to Boulder as he sits in front of the Boulder County Courthouse each day, cross-legged, smiling at people. He interacts with passersby and city and county employees, chatting and catching up. It is clear that he is a fixture, but no one quite understands how he got here or why.

"It's a way of life. I've lived in shelters in Denver, the Bay Area, New York, Connecticut, Boston and now

> "I like to read so I often go to the library and read the dictionary."

Boulder. My mom, sister and younger brother live in New York where I grew up. My next older brother is in Chicago."

"Would you ever want to go back to teaching?" I asked.

"It might be that I'm teaching now," he said in a slightly provocative way. "A lot of this is in my book, *A Transient's Guide to the Universe*, that I wrote in 1996. It's in the Library of Congress. My next book is *Chess: An Autobiographical Novel*. It's in my head."

Ed covers a great many topics: The antagonists in the Federal system, the stigma of mental illness and homelessness and George Will's interesting article on that subject, his work in "several banks," Bill Clinton's political path and that Hillary Clinton was in law school at Yale when he was there as an undergraduate.

I found it difficult to follow his thought process. Though he demonstrated a broad vocabulary and articulate phrases, there were many "blank spots" in his conversation.

"What do you find are the advantages to living on the street?"

"You are your own person. Simplicity. People like to feel special."

"What would you want mainstream people to know?"

I inquired.

"Mainstream," he repeats thoughtfully, "mainstream (pause) I don't have a problem with 'stream' or 'main.'..." He clearly didn't like the connotation of "mainstream." I dropped it.

"Do you see your family very often?"

"No. Financially that's not really feasible but my brother in Chicago writes me and sends me money."

Ed said he has a box at the Boulder Post Office. "My mother writes me regularly."

Ed closed our interview quoting Willie Nelson's lyrics from "Opportunity to Cry:"

It's been a long night so I think I'll go home
and feed my nightmares.
They've been waiting all night long
They'll be the last ones to tell me goodbye.

Cody

Cody

by Kate Guilford

"Yesterday was one of the best days of my life. Everything just lined up. I was very humbled by the world. ... I'm really grateful for everything that happens to me. Like this [interview] today. This is great. Thank you all for doing this."

Cody, an engaging 20-year-old from the Midwest, grew up in the suburbs and started studying Buddhism when he was 17. His passion for life is contagious. He's a traveler, and at the time of this interview had been in Boulder four days. He knew where to find free food, clothing and meditation groups, where to sleep and where not to. He is resourceful. Cody is more houseless than homeless. He can return to his parents' home if he wants.

"I'm not sure why I came to Boulder, but I'm sure glad to be here. Everything has just lined up like a big beautiful flower. I'm so content with my life right now. There's even a Buddhist college here. Naropa's wonderful; so much good spiritual energy here. I've never had friends that were into Buddhism."

"Walking is one of my favorite things to do. It gives me time to think. ... At night I try to recap each day. Sometimes it's hard because every day is filled with so much adventure. Each morning I think, what's going to happen today?"

"It's like, I don't get serious about money. When it comes to things that you need, life gives you what you need. A lot of times you're sitting there and it practically drops right in front of you, and you're just like, 'Wow! What do you know? Exactly what I need, like, how convenient.' How beautiful this world is because it just like works out, you know. Everything's always all right. You know, shit happens, there's suffering. It sucks and all, but it's like, OK. It's gonna be OK. If there wasn't suffering there wouldn't be happiness. Happiness comes from the cessation of suffering. ... Since all life is suffering all life has the potential for happiness."

"I don't 'spange' (spare change) much; now and then, mostly for the experience." Holding up a black Sharpie pen, he said, "This is a hippie credit card. I was thinking of making a funny sign today. Something like, 'Happy Hippie Stuck on Stupid.'"

Asked what he is serious about, he said, "I'm serious about keeping things calm; keeping the peace. I'm serious about food." His deep brown eyes twinkled behind his glasses.

"In Buddhism there's room for everything, you know. Just don't cause anybody any suffering, and you can do whatever you want. True freedom ... don't cause any harm. That's simple. That's easy. That's real easy to do." Pulling a well-worn book from his pocket, Cody said, "I have a handwritten copy of the Diamond Sutra [a classic Buddhist text]."

"We're all people. People set up bubbles around

[themselves]. Set up their cage. No one is allowed to break the barriers. That's what I'm out to do. I'm out to break the barriers that people set up. I walk down the street and I smile, and I try to make eye contact with everyone. That's one of the most important things, I think. I try to be real friendly. I wave and say 'Howdy' to people and stuff. A lot of people are just happy to get a smile, you know."

"Just like any group of people that you find, there are [homeless] people who are really nice, and there are people who are really mean; people who are compassionate and people who are self-centered. Any group of people you take, it's like that. But when it comes to travelers and home bums [homeless people who stay in one place] and stuff, a lot of them are pretty nice, share and stuff.

"The best part of being a traveler is the connections; the way everything works out. It's like this happens here, and this happens over here, and because these things happen, three other things happen. It fractals out into this big, beautiful flower and all the points

> "I'm not sure why I came to Boulder, but I'm sure glad to be here."

connect. And it turns into a big beautiful mandala that is our perceived reality, you know. Our now, our here. It's all about connections. People you meet, things you do, energy you transmit into the world and energy you receive. . . . You just gotta give a good energy out to the world."

"I don't get into conflicts. I'm pretty intuitive. I pick up easily on changing energy. When things start getting tense, I leave. Let's give peace a chance."

Cody's journey strikes me as being similar to those of people who bum around places like Europe, South America or Southeast Asia after high school. He's traveling and searching, getting to know himself and the world. These lyrics from a song he wrote say it best:

Some may call me homeless.
I like to think of it as home free.
If you're homeward bound
Then you're bound to home,
And that's just not the life for me.

Dan

Dan

by Mandy Walker

Dan is 38 and has been homeless for about seven years in the Denver/Boulder area. Dan has a history of anger management problems aggravated by a severe brain injury from a car crash almost 20 years ago, which also left him suffering from seizures. His anger means he has a history of violence, a history he's now working hard to end.

Here's Dan:

Flying [the street term for standing on a street corner holding a sign asking for money] was an interesting thing at first. My buddy John, we call him "Long Past Hungry" because that's what his sign used to say, he was the one that got me started. John said, "It's easy. Pretty much you just stand there with a sign on the corner and wait." You learn how to work the traffic, to walk back and forth along the cars, to make sure everyone sees your sign. I always look people in the eye, even when I'm wearing my sunglasses, because people like to look you in the eyes. When they're going to give you money, they want to see your eyes.

I feel sorry for people when they don't give me money because I know it's going to come back on them. That's the way life seems to work. I didn't understand that for a long time but in the last few years, I've been more committed myself. ...I don't have any specified religion or anything. ... I'm a Christian, I believe in God and I believe in Jesus. Ever since I got into talking to God more and making it more a part of my life, things have gotten a lot better for me.

Whether they realize it or not, everyone who drives by you on the corner, every one of them is being judgmental. Even some of the ones who give money are being judgmental. They look at you and they're classifying you, putting you in a group, and that's wrong. That's just the way life and people are. If we knew how to change that, it'd be a lot easier to make the world a better place.

God talks to me a lot. A lot of times when I'm walking along and I ask for something, sometime shortly after that, I'll get it. I used to sometimes wonder if God could even hear me, but when you say stuff like, "Well, if you could really do this," and it actually happens.

I do read the Bible somewhat. Every day I try to open it up to a random spot and read a few sections. It's kind of weird. My father always said I was a little bit different, especially from my four sisters. He always wanted a son and I was the only one he got. He always told me that I was special to God and that if I didn't realize that before it got too late, I was going to lose that. I wasn't quite sure what he meant until I started getting older.

> Getting that close to killing somebody, I was afraid I'd stepped over the line.

I don't go to church or anything like that, but I don't think any of us have to. Our relationship with God should be on our own personal level. All the religions are going to intermix in some way because almost all religions, no matter what worship they have, almost all of them believe there is a higher power that made everything.

My parents named me Daniel out of the Bible, which I guess makes me happy because I've died over a dozen times and I'm still here, so apparently, like my father told me after my car accident, when I died three times in the ambulance, "God's got you here for a purpose. You need to realize that he's warning you. He's not going to give you too many warnings like this." But he's given me several so far and it finally made me change my lifestyle.

It's pretty easy to get into conflicts just being alive, but since I've made a conscious choice not to get into conflicts as much anymore, I think my attitude has changed.

One of the things that helped was the last knife fight I got in. This guy asked me to step outside the fence. When we got down by the river, he already had a knife in his hand and I pulled out a razor knife. He got close to me and I sliced his throat open, right across his jugular and his esophagus, but right after I did that,

I just kind of looked at the knife and I threw it down. Eventually he threw his knife down and we wound up punching each other a few times.

Getting that close to killing somebody, I was afraid I'd stepped over the line. I knew it would come close to that point eventually. I was happy I didn't go that deep on him and I was happy I threw the knife down. It was a slap in the face for me, a little wake-up, "What are you doing?"

Whenever I get angry, my rage goes straight to the point of wanting to kill somebody. That's something you've got to learn how to control. It's hard to walk away from a fight.

One day recently I got really mad at somebody out here and started walking away from the guy. I was like, "God, you really got to help me now. This guy really just pissed me off. I want to hurt him." All God asked me was, "Why are you mad?"

Then I just stopped. He made me stop and realize that I didn't know why I was mad. It made me think about my anger more that way. It made me wonder how many other times I've gotten really aggravated and almost tried to kill somebody over nothing, like spilling some water or something small like that.

God's a good friend to have around.

Frank

by Tom deMers

"I was parked as far back into the hills by the hospital as you could get," Frank said. "Sleeping up there on the floor of my truck with a knee injury, freezing, not knowing where I would get food or how I could start my life again. My attitude was, "Screw society, screw mankind. No one's to be trusted, myself included. In truth, I probably would have gotten frostbite and died, been attacked by an animal or God knows what. But that's where my head was. I'm truly dropping out. I'll eat nuts. My desperation will lead me to find the right roots. I don't know what I was thinking."

"Then Mental Health picked me up and said, you can't do that. And I go, 'Why? Why can't I just regress like a wild animal?' That's when I was referred into Walnut Place [Boulder Housing Partners, City of Boulder's public housing program]."

With housing in place, Frank began to heal through counseling from the Center for People with Disabilities. Post-traumatic stress disorder had caught up with him, the result of brutal, physical abuse by a violent, alcoholic father. His physical scars served as a daily reminder. "Six months before, I was a white-collar banker," he said. "It was a radical shift for me."

Snap pictures of Frank before and after Walnut Place and, like an advertisement for a weight loss product, you see the difference. Before, Frank was homeless, sleeping in his pickup truck, paranoid and desperately trying to survive. After, he emerges like Superman from a phone booth, exuding optimism, looking thoughtfully back on his homeless years.

Frank credits the Sister Carmen Community Foundation with teaching him new ways of thinking and communicating. In their Bridges Out of Poverty course he learned to turn away deliberately from traumatic memories that lead toward depression. "At first," he said, "it feels unnatural to tune in to optimism. It takes daily affirmations and conscious effort to create the mindset that leads to happiness." He added, smiling, "Now I simply let the emotional storms go, like bad weather passing through."

Frank said that Adult Children of Alcoholics was another group supporting his transition. "Anyone can benefit by practicing AA's famous Twelve Steps."

In his new housing, his entrepreneurial spirit led him to start a "breakfast club" and he discovered purpose in helping others, many with conditions far worse than his.

He left Walnut Place after three years, with a Section 8 Housing Program voucher, and enrolled at Front Range Community College. There he was president

> "There is no map for your average poor person to cross the bridge from poverty to the middle class."

Frank

for two years of Students in Free Enterprise, a campus group that promotes business ethics. For his "capstone" graduation project, Frank created a community service organization with Richard Shane, a Denver psychologist and sleep therapist, to share the importance of sleep -- often neglected by college students. Frank created a Wiki where students could share insights about sleep and Shane offered free Sleep Easily CDs with sleep advice. In May 2011, Frank graduated magna cum laude with a degree in International Business, armed with excellent references about his personal leadership, he said.

"There is no map for your average poor person to cross the bridge from poverty to the middle class," Frank said. "There is this futility you face, not seeing a way out, just stuck there with your monthly check that you can barely live on, and you're staring at a world that can't see you and that you don't understand. So you acculturate to the habits of being poor. You bond with others at your same level, trapped by your own attitudes."

Frank observed that the poor spend their energy and time on entertainment while middle-class people are building strong relationships around information and business networking. He noticed major differences in values and language. Among the impoverished, Frank found frequent complaining and fingerpointing, a habit he believes is less prevalent in the middle class, where people want to create positive futures. "Words create the reality they express," Frank said. He now realizes the "kryptonite" that sapped his strength was his own depressed and hopeless attitude.

Today Frank is applying for jobs and writing a screenplay, a fantasy in which our Founding Fathers return to witness the results of their "Great Experiment."

"I am so happy to be where I am right now," he said. "I want to sing and dance but also give back to the community. I see a new chapter, a new lifestyle, ahead for me."

Michael P.

by Elle Page

We had taken Michael's picture months before but hadn't been able to catch up with him for an interview. We tracked him down in the Boulder County Jail. Michael is 6 feet, 10 inches tall and very slender. He had just awakened before he shuffled into the interview room in his striped uniform, and I felt sad as they handcuffed him.

Michael was born in Boulder in 1984 to a 16-year-old single mom. His dad, 21, left after two weeks. When he was 4, his mom married. His stepdad, he said, treated him as an outcast. "I was a different man's son."

At age 9, Michael's pattern of running away began and he was often gone for months at a time. "I rebelled against my mom. I was expelled. I lived for a while with my grandparents in New Jersey." He sought emancipation and ended up in several different group homes. Of those group homes, he praised Community Care in Englewood as "the best ever!"

At 16, Michael said he was given four shots to drink of what friends told him was Everclear grain alcohol, but it turned out to be "LSD wash." In his ensuing drugged state, Michael jumped into a tree and was making monkey sounds when the police arrived; they gave him his nickname, Monkey, which he still uses. He was addicted to meth and heroin at that same age. "I

> "I get too bored living inside, too closed up. You have to pay rent."

even OD'd [overdosed] a couple of times. I don't let the drugs control me. I don't steal. I just use drugs socially." He explained, "I had no male who disciplined me."

At 19, Michael hitchhiked to New Jersey to try to live with his mom, who was divorced. She lived next door to her parents, who were taking care of her due to her multiple system atrophy, a degenerative neurological disorder. Michael ended up in Atlantic City and worked at a Denny's restaurant.

One night he got into an argument with a roommate who happened to belong to the East Side Bloods gang. "I didn't hold my tongue," he said. "I was just a hippie kid from Boulder and they thought I was like the Columbine shooter since I wore a trench coat." He said gang members beat him and left him out in the cold with a brain hemorrhage. The doctor told Michael that he was lucky it was 18 degrees that night. If it had been 20 degrees he would have died, he said. "That's when I got this," Michael said, pointing to the tattoo on his neck that says "20".

Recovering in the hospital, Michael was diagnosed with borderline paranoid schizophrenia and was sent to a mental hospital. Then his mom sent him back to Boulder, where she thought he could get help and would be safer.

Michael P.

"I didn't want to do the living indoors thing. I wanted to party and sell meth again. I got a bunch of high school kids addicted to meth and my friends hated me for it. I wasn't thinking right. I quit meth cold turkey on my twenty-first birthday." But at age 22 he said he was "busted for possession of meth and got my first felony."

"I get too bored living inside, too closed up. You have to pay rent. If I lived indoors I'd have to sell drugs to pay rent, so I decided to live outside."

At one point Michael said he was suicidal. He tried to hang himself but he thought, "I can't do this in front of my dog." He got another tattoo, "DGAF:" Don't Give A F___.

Why is he in jail now? As a joke, he said, he shot a friend with a plastic BB gun he found in a Dumpster. While the friend laughed, someone else called the police. He was to get out of jail in a week. "What will you do?" I asked.

"I might go to school to occupy my time and get an RV. I'll keep doing drugs. I like how they make me feel and I'm more motivated when on drugs." Then he shared a purpose: "I like to help runaways. I turn them in to the police. It's not a good place to be on the streets. They need to go home."

"What do you regret?"

"All the trouble I've gotten myself into, two felonies and a ton of misdemeanors. It'll be hard if I ever want to live inside."

"What are your strengths?"

His first answer: "I'm an a__hole. I let people know how annoying they really are. I like the shock value. If they can handle it, they're my friends." Then, remembering the question, "I'm loyal. Forgiving. Too trusting. Strong – I sleep outside in negative degrees. There's only five of us who truly sleep on the street all winter. I don't sleep in shelters 'cause I feel boxed in, like jail."

At the end of the interview, Michael made a poignant statement. Two days after his 18th birthday the state closed the Community Care facility he loved, for budget reasons. "I would have stayed until I was 21," he said. "Things might have been different if I had."

The Women

Life on the streets is challenging and dangerous for women. They do what they can to disguise their vulnerability and protect themselves from exploitation and trauma.

A recent study in Massachusetts reported that 92 percent of homeless women had experienced severe physical or sexual assault at some point in their life. Sixty-three percent were victims of violence by an intimate partner.
— National Alliance to End Homelessness Fact Checker, 2007
National Coalition for the Homeless, Fact Sheet #7, August 2007

Hope

Hope

by Curtine Metcalf

Hope's journey to homelessness began at age 12 when she had to choose between life and the severe abuse she suffered at the hands of her alcoholic parents. For Hope, leaving was survival. She was a "military brat" whose parents followed frequent new assignments. Getting by and raising herself from the age of 12, she left for Hollywood at 15, a familiar dream for young people. When a friend was shot, and died in her arms, she quickly learned, she said, that life on her own also harbored great danger.

Hope has been in Boulder for about six months. Boulder is much more accepting and has many more resources for the homeless population than most other cities, she said. One crucial factor for Hope is the fact that her beloved dog, Baby, can be with her at the Boulder Shelter for the Homeless. Baby is her shadow. Not only is she her constant companion, she also 'gets' Hope. Hope said she has been diagnosed with bi-polar/manic depressive disorder and post-traumatic stress disorder. When Hope thrashes about during post-traumatic nightmares, Baby gently paws her to wake her from her trauma. Baby senses when Hope is in a pre-bipolar state of mind and very calmly "takes charge when she thinks she needs to," explained Hope.

Baby, who also came from an abusive early life, keeps Hope putting one foot in front of the other every day. Non-judgmental, and nurtured in unconditional love, the magic is visible in the unspoken communication between these two. They are both alive, together, and making a better life. They rescued each other.

Seeking the often-elusive loving family, children and a stable life, Hope has been married three times. Lacking a healthy mental and emotional role model for marriage, she divorced twice to get out of bad situations. Her last marriage ended when her husband couldn't deal with her health and medication issues. So she and her two youngest children were turned out on the street, she said. Her children were later put in foster care because of their homelessness. The words of one of her children echo in her head, "Mommy, I'll come find you."

She is soon to be 40, and her five kids, who are 18, 17, 11, and 8-year-old twins, are in other, safe places. She knows she cannot care for them right now. With a proud sparkle in her eye, she showed photos of her kids and said she maintains contact with her 17-year-old on Facebook.

With mental health issues that continually present a challenge, Hope appreciates the health options available to her in Boulder. She sees a therapist regularly through Boulder County Mental Health, stays on her medications and meets each day as it comes. Asked what a good day looks like, Hope said, "I'm still alive. I may not be the healthiest person around, but I make

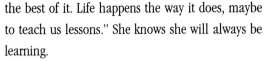

the best of it. Life happens the way it does, maybe to teach us lessons." She knows she will always be learning.

Hope is an attractive, clean and well-put-together woman. She noted that people find it odd that she has manners. Hope has been stereotyped in a group of people not always regarded as polite, clean or working to make their way out of the homeless dilemma. Hope does not drink or do street drugs, has no record with the law and has never been in jail. She doesn't want to do anything that encourages the community or world to give up on the homeless, a prevalent feeling that she and others fight daily. It is a stigma that follows her.

Hope has dreams: she wants to have a permanent home, a supportive sweetheart and companion, and her children close to her. She keeps her creative side alive and well. A published writer of short stories, she journals regularly and hopes to someday own a ceramic shop where she and others can practice their art and let their creative sides run wild.

Asked what she believes in, Hope said, "Karma, a Higher Power and much Native American wisdom."

"What goes around comes around and I am accepting of that. Life is what you make of it." Hope wanted others to know that "not all homeless are bad, not all are drunks and so many are just trying to make it."

Her most prized possession? "That four-legged Baby," of course.

Of all the things Hope doesn't have, one thing she gives thanks for daily and wears without hesitation is her own sense of pure hope.

> **When Hope thrashes about during post-traumatic nightmares, Baby gently paws her to wake her from her trauma.**

Jade

by Deborah Fryer

Jade wants a home, but only under certain conditions. After a major mold exposure in 2007 she developed chemical sensitivities, so she can't live in a place with new carpeting or fresh paint. A two-bedroom place would be perfect, with enough privacy for the clients who come to her for trauma therapy and sexual healing.

As much as Jade yearns for a place to call her own, and as clear as her vision is for the home she wants, an equal measure of restlessness keeps her constantly on the move. "I have had trouble staying put," she said over a cup of herbal tea. "I have gypsy feet. I love to move around."

Even though she sold real estate off and on for 24 years in Austin, Texas, she has never owned a property. As a tenant, she said, she has taken impeccable care of every place she's lived and never lost a security deposit.

Jade has experienced "cycles of homelessness" since the late 1970s. She puts her things in storage and travels, visits friends, house-sits, couch-surfs and lives out of her car. "I used to say I was adventuring, or traveling or visiting people," she said, "but at 59, it's getting a lot harder. I am determined to break the pattern. To do that, I've had to own the label of being homeless." She put down her tea and looked out the window at the falling snow. "I am

> "I see myself as the one that came into the family system and said, 'Enough. We are going to heal these patterns of violence and abuse.'"

without a home," she said. Her voice trembled. "I'm staying in a friend's basement in Denver now and commuting to Boulder, working to find a place to live here."

Jade has tried to find a home through Boulder County's affordable housing program, but she says caseworkers don't understand her chemical sensitivities. It's not that she has no money: she runs monthly heart pujas, devotional ceremonies that attract up to thirty people every month. Jade believes that her bouts of homelessness happen because when she was a child, she learned that home was not a safe place to be.

"I was raised in a family that did not know how to express love," she said. "Home was not a place of nurturance, acceptance or kindness for me." When she was a little girl, she was sometimes locked out of her house for the day, so she had to pee in the bushes, drink out of the garden hose and eat tomatoes from the yard. "My mother was always hateful to me," she said. "I don't ever remember her touching me with love, it was always with impatience and criticism. Our family had every trauma in the book: insanity, war trauma, sexual abuse, murder, suicide. I see myself as the one that came into the family system and said, 'Enough. We are going to heal these patterns of violence and abuse.'"

Jade does not shy away from the truth. She moves toward it like a firewalker, determined to confront the hot coals of her past so they no longer have control over her present life. She speaks with purpose and eloquence. She is sensitive, compassionate, open, generous. She doesn't use alcohol or drugs. You won't find her in a shelter. The only night she stayed in one, she developed a rash from exposure to the bleached sheets. She is one of the invisible homeless who ekes out her living the best way she can, with an amazing amount of love and trust for humanity, even after all she has been through.

She seems to care very much about helping people. "I believe that trauma is the foundation of all mental illness," she said. One of the ways she acted out the sexual abuse of her childhood was to work as a prostitute, she said, retiring at age 36. "I was suited for it. And believe it or not, it was healing for me because I felt I was providing a needed service. I felt valued, and had some clients for 10 years." She views her past as a foundation for the work she does now: promoting love, healing and healthy expressions of intimacy and sexuality.

"I really appreciate everything that has brought me to this moment. It has all made me who I am," she said.

But for all her appreciation and awareness, all of her compassion, she is still homeless.

"What do you think is in the way of you settling down?" I ask her. "What is stopping you?"

Her eyes well up. She sighs. The tears spill over her cheeks and she doesn't bother to wipe them away.

"There is a deep, core part of me, installed by the wounding from my mother, which says I don't deserve stability, safety or comfort. There's a fear I won't be able to take care of myself. My deepest fear is that I am unlovable."

Editor's Note: *After almost two years of homelessness, Jade found a place to live with the help of Boulder County's emergency housing program. She vowed to clear the trauma that has caused the cycles of homelessness in her life, so that she is never homeless again.*

Katie

Katie

by Eliza Cross

"As soon as the sun rises, I get up and get going," said Katie, a lovely blonde 32-year-old artist who lives on the streets. Earlier this year Katie was an award-winning art student living in a Boulder apartment. Today she's "on the road," "residentially challenged" or "on a European backpack tour," some of the euphemisms she said homeless people use jokingly to describe their living status.

On Friday the 13th, in May 2011, Katie was evicted from her apartment after her brother stole the rent money she had hidden in a drawer. She said she went straight to the streets, sleeping behind a Dumpster during her first night without a bed.

When she reported the theft to police, her brother — who she said already had two felony convictions — threatened to kill her. Efforts to reclaim her money were largely in vain, since she said the police never followed up or called her back. "I quickly learned that the police don't really take you seriously if you're homeless," Katie said.

Law enforcement officials weren't the only ones who dismissed her because of her living status, Katie said. "A cut I'd gotten on my leg became infected after I tried to bathe in the creek. At the hospital, they just assumed I was there trying to get drugs

> "Most people living on the street have had awful things happen to them, and yet they'll do anything for you."

— even though I've never done hard drugs in my life. I've never felt so profiled. God forbid you should have dreadlocks or mismatched clothes if you want law enforcement or hospitals to take you seriously. When you're homeless, no one listens to you."

Not so long ago Katie had an iPhone and a laptop, she said, but now she relies primarily on free computer time at a coffee house or library to communicate. "It wasn't easy to go from being completely connected to being unplugged from technology," she said. "But now I realize how disconnected people really are when they're so busy texting, Facebooking and e-mailing all the time. In a way, it's freeing to be away from it."

The dangers for a single woman on the street are many, and Katie has learned to trust her instincts. "I get a feeling about people and I pay attention," she said. "When I've ignored my inner voice, that's when I've gotten in trouble. I've learned to listen to my intuition about choosing where to sleep at night, and I usually wait until after it gets dark to find a place that's out of the way." One night in Boulder when it was raining, she and a friend slept inside a dumpster. "He taught me to look for the recycling symbol when you're trying to find a dumpster to sleep in, because hopefully it's just filled with paper and cardboard, and no smelly garbage."

She describes panhandling as a necessary but degrading endeavor. "I'm independent and I don't like asking for money, but when you need help, you need help," she said. "It's embarrassing and horrible, so I just try to make people laugh. If you can get a smile out of somebody, it's better than nothing." When people respond unkindly, she tries not to take it personally. "I just wish people could learn to love people more," she said. "For all I know, one of those people who looked down on me might be out on the streets himself someday. And when he comes asking me for something, you know what? I'll still help him."

Katie seems determined to find the good in her situation. "Last March, if you had told me this was going to happen I would have thought that I'd die being out on the street. I've lost so many things that once seemed important to me. But now if you dropped me in a foreign country with two dimes in my pocket, I know I could survive."

She thinks people would be surprised at the depth of most of the homeless. "Home bums are some of the best people I've ever met," she said. "Most people living on the street have had awful things happen to them, and yet they'll do anything for you. They'll give you the shirt off their back, even if they don't know where they're going to get another shirt. Karma is more real than I ever knew, and I've learned that if you put out good energy, you get good energy back."

In the future, Katie hopes to combine her passion for art with helping kids. "Someday I'd love to do art therapy for children and families that are in transition, maybe at a place like the Carriage House Community Table," she said. "I'd like to help the younger generation discover their natural gifts and talents."

She also hopes to have a home again. Katie's voice broke as she said, "It's a conundrum, because so many good things and so many bad things can happen in the same day, but you have to find the positive. Some mornings I awaken with the sunrise and I feel fortunate, because most people never get to fully experience the light and warmth from the sun."

Joy D.
by Joy Eckstine

Joy is strong at the broken places. She describes a family racked with addiction and brutality, a family where she was punished for speaking the truth of her perceptions. Her family moved every year and had cut ties with all extended family. Searching for a different life, Joy's mother was trying to escape the terrible abuse that had marred her life. If there was a problem with a job or a school, Joy's family moved on. They taught her, "Don't look back."

Bright but dyslexic, stubborn and resilient, Joy graduated from high school at 16. She attended college for two years, at school during the day and working as a hostess at two different Best Westerns at night. She drove 60 miles each way to a different location in order to earn money to survive. "I didn't sleep for a few years!" she said. Joy left college because she felt that she didn't fit in, and returned home to take care of her mother, who had developed cancer. She was asked to leave when she was 19 years old, in part because of her employment plans.

Her decision to attend beauty school brought derision from her family and they refused to help her in any way, telling her that beauty school was "not respectable" and "low class." After she was asked to leave home, she had no idea where to go or what to do. Resources like craigslist and e-mail did not yet exist and Joy was very isolated. She began sleeping in her van and got a health club membership so that she could shower. She lost her job at Best Western because beauty school often went late, making her late for work too many times.

Some other women at the school noticed her van and invited her to share an apartment, telling her where to find a job that paid much better than Best Western. It was at a strip club, and although she never "danced" there, she made excellent money and graduated from beauty school. She said she never needed to trade sex for safety or shelter but that she saw innumerable women who made this bargain. About women's homelessness, she said, "It just depends on who is in your life — your resources and their resources."

She launched her career as a hairdresser and has never looked back.

Joy's family didn't know her secret homelessness, but she knows their secrets and she speaks to break the chains of shame that surround incest, violence and addiction in families. Although the beatings she experienced were brutal, she said they taught her the most important lessons in her life — that one's value is not based on others' perceptions.

> Her decision to attend beauty school brought derision from her family and they refused to help her in any way ...

Joy

This has sustained her through deprivation, through the struggles of a single woman business owner, and even through national controversy when she dyed her poodle pink a few years ago in support of breast cancer fundraising and was ticketed by the police.

Joy spoke passionately about how women in poverty often must use their sexuality to survive, exchanging it for shelter, for protection, to get work and for access to privileges that they are otherwise denied, and for the numbness of drugs that allow them to continue the barter of their bodies.

Joy eschews drugs and those with the self-destructive haunting of drugs so clearly displayed in their eyes.

She has worked hard amid the continuing rejection and abuse from her family, lovers who disappoint and betray and even friends who do not understand the demanding hours that a woman alone must work.

Standing proudly in her gleaming studio, with pouting lips, sparkling makeup, and colorful flowered tattoos down her arms, Joy speaks her truth and reminds us that it is the death of your soul to be anything but true to yourself. "Homelessness has nothing to do with your IQ, your desire for survival or your ability to work," she said. "It's merely a series of events your soul has chosen to experience."

Jane
by Kristin Pazulski

Seeing Jane at the Boulder Public Library, one would never place her with the homeless population that spends time there. Dressed neatly in jeans, a sweatshirt and playful, multicolored gloves, her graying hair tied up in a looped bun, Jane looks like any middle-aged woman checking her e-mail or reading news websites. But Jane's online perusal is not for entertainment. She is sitting at the computer applying for jobs. Again. Her time in the library is as much a productive distraction as it is an effort to avoid winter's freezing temperatures. And behind her normal façade lies a constant nagging worry — where I am sleeping tonight?

Jane, who has been without a steady home for a year and a half, has never had to "camp," or sleep on the streets, in any literal sense; every morning she wakes up, though, knowing that this night could be the first. Jane, 44, originally from Minnesota, has been spending her winter nights at the Boulder Shelter for the Homeless but during previous homeless stints she has spent time in many of Denver's shelters and some of the city's transitional housing programs. She has an income of $140 a month from Aid to the Needy and Disabled, a state cash assistance program, and receives $180 in food stamps per month. Residual pain from work-related carpal tunnel and a

car accident in 2005 left her unable to look for work until recently, but so far her resumes have yielded no response.

Her days begin around 6 a.m., when she packs her backpack, finishes her chores and leaves the Boulder Shelter for the Homeless. There is no lounging in pajamas, sipping a coffee or starting her day on her own terms. The rush to get out by 8 a.m. is followed by a short bus ride into Boulder. When there is no bus, she and others from the shelter walk the five miles into town. Not a big deal on a spring day, but winter is another story.

Some mornings it's hard to get up, she said, knowing that a day full of dirty looks and disrespect, paperwork and seemingly endless resume sending awaits. "I'll have days where I wake up and I'm like, I can't do this again today. I can't go out there and face the weather and the people and the uncertainty and the stress and [getting] all this stuff done in a very crowded, distracted environment."

At the moment she is working on getting a new ID card, applying for jobs and trying to figure out why Aid to the Needy and Disabled paid her too much. Most of the time she finds help at the Carriage House Community Table's day room, and when she needs

> "That need for security ... is just so blasted out of the water when you're outside on your own."

Jane

an escape from there, she goes for walks in Boulder. When she needs to warm her hands she goes to the bus terminal, although security officers often ask her and others to move on.

Jane said being homeless as a woman is much different than it is for a man. "I think there's a fear factor, a vulnerability that women have that men don't," she said. "Women like the comforts of home, and we like to be warm, and we like to be clean. That need for security that I think most women have is just so blasted out of the water when you're outside on your own." She's been asked by men if she'd be interested in sleeping with them for payment, and she has seen many women "hook up" with a man simply because they are lonely.

Employment for homeless women, she said, is tougher, too. "As far as finding employment. ... I believe that in some ways it is easier for men because they are much more able to perform physical labor,"

which while short-term and temporary, pays well. "There is also the obstacle of criminal backgrounds [Jane has a previous criminal arrest]. "People who hire men for physical labor aren't as likely to check a background or worry about drug use due to the work being short-term. That's been my observation."

Nor can women usually turn to other women to create a sense of home and security, since relationships are temporary and inconsistent. "The bonding among the women in the shelters …doesn't happen, unlike other group settings [military, workplace] where women are grouped together like that."

So the library is Jane's hideaway, a place to get away from the bustle of the crowd at the Carriage House Community Table, the cold of winter and the glares from people who don't understand who she is and why she is there.

Debbie

Debbie

by Lori Batcheller

Each morning Debbie wakes up before sunrise to the sound of birds chirping outside her tent in the mountains west of Boulder. Her neighbors are mountain lions, foxes, a mother bear and her cub, and Debbie likes it that way. Most days she heads into Boulder, usually catching a ride with someone from Nederland, and interacts with her homeless community.

Debbie considers herself the information kiosk for the newly homeless, instructing them where they can get food and clothing. "There's no reason to go hungry in Boulder," she said, speaking with pride when she mentions mentoring friends to help them get off welfare.

Debbie's plunge into the homeless community happened relatively recently. For 20 years she was a suburban housewife raising her two children, and living what many would consider the good life.

"I lived in a nice five-bedroom home in Conifer and we owned five cars," said Debbie. "My husband had a good job with an automobile company and we went to company Christmas parties at the Red Lion Inn." Originally from Chicago, Debbie's father was the vice president of a record company. Debbie holds an associate's degree in business management with a 4.0 grade average, and at one time worked as a veterinary technician.

All that changed in 2005 when her 26-year-old daughter's life ended tragically.

"Things went into the toilet," said Debbie, a reasonably nicely dressed middle-aged woman with loose blond curls. Along with other necklaces, bracelets and rings she's been given over the years, she wears a necklace that her remaining daughter sent her from Portland. Debbie said she tries to dress nicely and just signed up for a shower at the Carriage House Community Table.

"When I lost Niki I went into shock and felt numb," Debbie said. To stay numb she turned to drugs, taking heroin, smoking crack and doing meth for about six months. "It was a hard six months," she admitted. And her troubles weren't over. Her husband suffered a head injury from a motorcycle accident and it took eight months for him to recover. Even then he couldn't hold down a job and ended up on disability. "We lost everything we owned," Debbie said.

In 2008 Debbie's husband divorced her and she and her remaining daughter moved into a group home. "It was a very, very bad time," she said. Debbie found an apartment but was later evicted, becoming one of Boulder's homeless. Ironically, for a while she lived under a bridge across from her husband's former employer.

Even before her daughter committed suicide — Debbie believes she was murdered — Debbie faced some challenges. She has been on disability since 1999 due to multiple health issues, including bipolar disorder. She became diabetic from medications and at one time became addicted to medications for chronic pain. She has fibromyalgia, degenerative joint disease, high blood pressure, neuropathy in her hands and feet and is legally blind secondary to cataracts. Her monthly disability payment is barely enough to buy essentials like her tent and camping gear.

The last few years have been a "big blur" she said, but Debbie knows she's the same worthwhile person she was when she lived in a nice house. Since becoming homeless, or "house-less" as she calls it, she has lost 20 pounds, her blood pressure is under control and she doesn't take any pain drugs, not even Tylenol.

"For 20 years she was a suburban housewife raising her two children, and living what many would consider the good life."

Debbie believes her experience has helped her become a better person. She now values friendship more than anything. "I realize that what's most important in life are not the things you own but the people around you.

When you don't own anything, people aren't trying to get anything from you. You learn who your true friends are." She said she tries not to judge anyone, that no one lives life without doing something they regret.

What bothers Debbie most is the attitude of the people who aren't homeless. "I get watched when I walk into a store that I used to spend $2,000 in and I'm now treated like a person who's not worthy," she said. "I used to have everything society thinks you should have, and now because I don't have all the material things, I'm treated differently."

If Debbie could do it all again, she would not have taken the drugs to ease her grief after losing her daughter. "I neglected to take care of things," she said, "and I regret not taking advantage of the opportunities I had."

Debbie wants people to understand that the homeless are not criminals, drug addicts or thieves. "Bad things happened that brought us here," she said. "Anyone can be here."

Helene Hope

by Marsha J. Perlman

"My friends call me 'Mayor of Boulder Creek,'" Hope, the name she prefers, said, laughing. "When kids come through here, I let them know where to eat and get a shower, where to sleep and what's to do here. Boulder is my home town!" She smiled with pride.

Then when they're settled in, she tells the newcomers, "You have to do some footwork to get off the streets. There are people to help you, but not to do it for you."

In the 1980s Hope lived in Boulder, in a trailer park. Then, with her husband, she moved to southern Colorado. After he died, she and her daughters returned to Boulder because they had loved it here.

Exuding stamina and courage, Hope and her youngest daughter have been living in public housing for five years. "While waiting for my application to move through the system, we lived on the streets for a year," she said. "We slept outdoors, sometimes 'couch surfing.' In the process, I learned the commitment of keeping appointments, following written and spoken directions, filling out required forms and working closely with caseworkers to gather information such as birth certificates."

She knows that the government's requirements and slow pace are difficult for many homeless. "Some don't have the patience, physical or mental stamina or ability to remember what they need to do and when. It's a tough situation."

Hope worked for many years as a housekeeper to buy food and pay her bills. "When I developed a slipped disk and osteoporosis, I could no longer do hard physical work."

Believing that her continued exertion would cause an irreparable slipped disk, Hope's doctor completed all required forms for her disability qualification.

"There are lots of criteria for available funds and I've been waiting many months for their decision," she said.

Hope expressed pride in her three daughters. The oldest has an associate degree and an infant and plans to return to school to become a registered nurse. Her middle daughter, a musician, is studying to be a special education teacher. The youngest, the only one remaining at home, will graduate from Boulder Preparatory High School, a charter school, in May.

"What about Hope?" I asked. "I'm studying online for an associate degree in human services from the University of Phoenix," she said with exuberance. "Then I'll be able to do more for the needy and homeless, like help in the churches and at the Carriage House Community Table." At present she's taking

> "You have to do some footwork to get off the streets. There are people to help you, but not to do it for you."

an involuntary hiatus from her education, citing 'no money for tuition,' She's waiting to receive disability payments.

As a strong and resourceful mother, 51-year-old Hope believes she has set her children along a proper path.

"They know that no matter what happens in life, they can move through it. They don't have to get into drugs or trouble."

Hope acknowledged that 10 years ago her daughters had problems in Boulder because of the city's generally affluent culture. "Kids with money looked down on those who had little," she said. "It was difficult, but the experience taught them about people, and to appreciate having a home, a dinner and a shower." She moved her girls from the ridicule into another school in hopes of a more accepting environment.

Because Hope doesn't know how to play an instrument or sing for donations on the Pearl Street Mall, she stands on a corner, "but only when I really need to. My sign reads: 'I Was Told Never To Be Afraid To Ask.'"

People shout at her, "Go get a job," or close their car windows and secure their doors. "A few have even spit at me," she said, "but many fill my hand with bills or spare change, or say, 'Good luck to you.' Sometimes church people take me in and give me lunch. I'm

spiritual, I do believe in God and I have my prayers."

Hope believes Boulder people are scared. "They don't understand the homeless. They see 'Please Help Me' signage and have no idea what stresses homeless people face."

I asked Hope what she'd like Boulder people to know. Without pausing, she answered:

"We're not bad people.

"We've had hard-working lives.

"Most of us would work if we were able.

"We understand what's going on in the world.

"We get stuck in situations where we have to go out signing to make money, and it's not something we're doing for beer and alcohol."

Late one hot Saturday afternoon in August, I met up with colorfully dressed Hope at the crowded Pearl Street Mall and four women were sitting on a low brick wall, waiting their turn for Hope's skillful fingers. She wove bright colored threads and beads into a pencil-thin braid hanging down a shoulder-length head of thick black hair.

"I've been busy since I set up this morning, customers all day," she said. Tired but talkative, Hope had earned food money for herself and her daughter.

Gathering her plastic trays of supplies she said, "I'll be here again tomorrow."

Terri

Terri

by Terri Sternberg

Who is that person hidden in a sleeping bag under the bushes by Boulder Creek, beneath a tree near the library, or in a broken wheelchair in the parking garage? Is it someone whose existence for 16 years revolved around a house, two cherished cats, a garden with roses and herbs, a digital recording studio, an extensive library and every kitchen gadget known to mankind? Art, antiques, and statues to nourish the spirit?

Is it the same person who carved a successful career out of scales, arpeggios, and etudes, along with the minutiae of a classical music education? The same person who drove between San Francisco and Boulder each summer to play the violin in two seasonal orchestras and enjoyed whitewater kayaking?

It's me, but I am hardly the same. The last two years have added a layer of disbelief, confusion and frustration. I use every instinct and skill to find a safe place to sleep and navigate the alphabet soup of community resources (SSI, SSDI, BCHS, BCHP, BCHA, BOHO, AARRGGHH!!!) Normal, petty difficulties regularly snowball into formidable nemeses.

What happened? When did the crippling depression that orchestrated the loss of my home set in? A date

> I use every instinct and skill to find a safe place to sleep and navigate the alphabet soup of community resources.

occurs to me – the day I realized that after a year and a half in the financial services industry, having spent thousands of dollars on education and licensing for life insurance and securities investments, I had earned exactly $147. I was told to find another office to work through. My sweet, 16-year-old kitty passed away that same night.

For the next year I scarcely got out of bed, especially after I sprained my knee. I emptied the bulging mailbox onto the living room floor once a week and the unpaid bills piled up. Who cared? Half of my family had died.

To spare my knee, I ordered takeout instead of cooking, even though my resources were dwindling. My neighbor who helped me clean house had seemingly disappeared and empty bags and containers littered the floors. My house was in incredibly bad condition when I heard the people at my door: two from the Longmont Code Enforcement Division, two police officers and a therapist – presumably to help me through the trauma.

I know a lot about trauma. I have a severe case of PTSD, mostly from being tied up and blindfolded by a serial rapist for 4½ hours when I was 20 years old. No one knew much about PTSD back then. The forensic exam consisted of the doctor saying, "Yeah, it looks like you were raped." No rape crisis hotline, no referral to counseling. Fortunately, the perpetrator was caught and imprisoned.

I had just moved to a new city to attend music school on a full scholarship, I decided I would not let this ruin everything I had worked for, and I went on as though nothing had happened. In a shell of blind numbness I stifled all of the incomprehensible feelings of fear, rage, and loathing.

This worked for about 20 years and then things began falling apart. Anxieties that I had previously attributed to "stage fright" became overwhelming. I constantly obsessed about practicing my instrument and reviewed past performances in my head.

So now five uninvited strangers were pounding on my door, wandering through my house taking pictures — of the newspaper on the stove burner that hadn't been used in months, the trash and recyclables cluttering the floors with pathways only I knew, the gaping holes in the ceiling.

When I bought the house, it had a "new roof" as a selling point. It leaked the first time it rained. The roofer said, "It's not the roof, it's the skylights." The insurance person said, "We don't insure for shoddy workmanship." The leaks gradually grew into gaping holes with mold. The code-enforcement posse condemned my house of 16 years. They also took my 16-year-old black, twitchy-tailed kitty and killed him. ("He doesn't look so good…")

After bouncing among several different places

in shock, I wound up at the Boulder Shelter for the Homeless. After four days I was hospitalized with the "kennel cough" that abounds in that environment. When my 90 allotted nights at the shelter ran out, I spent my first night on the street. At first I enjoyed sleeping under the stars and falling asleep to the music of coyotes or the gurgling creek. But the times when sleep is impossible gradually build into an enervating, all-pervasive fog that competes with any available ounce of self-preservation. Everything I had owned had been stolen, confiscated or thrown away. Stints in jail for "camping," trespassing or "littering" wore on me further.

Homeless people die younger than most; their energy is worn down by everyday hardships, but also by sneering people whose unvoiced fear is probably that they, too, could become homeless. Almost anyone who owns something has a fear of losing it. And to hate or belittle someone who has lost everything is a great way of talking yourself into believing that it could never happen to you.

Well, it did happen. It happened to me.

The Families

Life can be less lonely with a family member or partner beside you. Family members can give you the strength to persevere, but can also introduce a greater sense of shame and worry.

Sixty percent of the homeless in Boulder in 2009 were individuals, 40 percent were part of a family. Of the families that were homeless in January 2009, 108 children were identified as ages 0-5.

— National Point in Time survey, January 2009

Eric and LeDriedre

Eric and LeDriedre

by Bunny Hender

LeDriedre and Eric were childhood friends who had no idea that their friendship would work to save both their lives.

Eric grew up in Denver and graduated from George Washington High School in 1978. After graduation, he moved to Texas to be with his girlfriend and started working as an electrician. They married and had a daughter, but the marriage didn't work, so in 1997 he moved back to Denver. Back in Colorado things began to go downhill and Eric began drinking, using and selling drugs and wound up in jail. When he got out he was homeless and still involved in drugs. He remembers one awful night when he had no place to go and was forced to sleep on a bench during a major snowstorm.

LeDriedre, or Didi, is another Denver native who has a similar story. She went through the Denver school system and as soon as she graduated she started having babies. She, too, was using drugs and as a single mother of four, she turned to selling to support her family. Once while she was in jail for a short time, she left the children with her mother, giving her enough money to pay the rent. When Didi got out, she found that her mother had used the rent money for drugs and Didi and her family were homeless. She managed to stay in a shelter and make enough money to find a new home for her family. Her children are grown now – all of them drug-free and working – but Didi will never forget the feeling of being on the street with four young children to care for.

Both Eric's and Didi's lives were filled with drugs and sadness when they happened to meet again in an alley during a drug deal. They renewed their friendship, which turned out to be good for both of them. Eric, a regular churchgoer, began to bring Didi to services with him and became friends with the clergyman, Pastor Bob. Eric and Didi were getting tired of the lives they were living, and Eric came up with a plan: Get out of Denver and away from the people who kept them connected to a life they didn't want. At first Didi didn't want to go but one day in February 2011, one of her friends turned on her, and she and Eric just packed up and left. Pastor Bob had told them about the Carriage House Community Table in Boulder and made the arrangements for them to go there.

Eric isn't sure why he came up with his plan when he did, but he is sure of one thing: People can't be forced to change – they have to be ready and they have to decide on their own to improve their lives. Eric and

> Both Eric's and Didi's lives were filled with drugs and sadness when they happened to meet again in an alley during a drug deal.

Eric and LeDreidre

Didi also feel strongly about their respect and appreciation for the Carriage House Community Table, which Eric calls "a great place."

"If people want to do better, the Carriage House will help," he said. "There's nothing I wouldn't do for them."

Since arriving at the Carriage House, both Eric and Didi have stopped drinking and using drugs. Didi, after applying for 27 jobs, was hired at a deli. Eric is working to get disability pay because of a spinal cord injury he sustained, and is currently cleaning and serving as an intern in the Carriage House Community Table. Joy, the executive director there, arranged to get the pair a condo of their own through the Homeless Prevention Rapid Rehousing Program. Didi said that having a roof over their heads with their names on the lease is one of the things she's proud of. On Father's Day Didi's children and grandchildren came over to Eric and Didi's new home for a barbecue and Eric did the grilling.

Eric was sick and tired of the life he was living. Didi believed in Eric and his plan. Because they had support and strength of character, the plan worked. Eric and Didi look forward to building a whole new life together.

Katrina and Dionshay

by Maryjo Faith Morgan

Katrina is a confident woman with an open smile. Her 4-year-old son climbs on and off her lap with easy familiarity. It is hard to believe they've been reunited only a few months. When she says his name, it sounds like music. Dionshay rolls from her mouth wrapped in a soft, almost French pronunciation, "Deé-aun-shā."

Katrina tells her story simply. Her speech is free of expletives; when repeating the acronym "BS" to quote others she says, "Excuse my language." She sprinkles "you know?" into her words as she describes her life without a home:

• You know, you want to get yourself together. You get tired of walking the streets.

• You know, they don't have places there [in Denver] really ... for women.

• I was coming up with different types of bugs; I really didn't like to stay in the shelters. They had bedbugs, lice, you know?

• So I was meeting people in the streets I didn't even know, and staying at their houses. That's not really safe either.

• But, you know, it was either that or stay on the streets … and freeze to death.

Listening to her, I cannot imagine having to find a safe place to sleep and ending up with lice. I cannot imagine how cold it must be, emotionally and physically, without a place to call home.

No. I do *not* know, Katrina.

Katrina makes no excuses, asks for no pity, places no blame. She mentions being taken from her mother at 2, becoming a ward of the state and countless foster homes. She met her mother again when she was 22.

"I wasn't a bad kid. Didn't steal cars or ditch school. I stayed at Excelsior [Youth Center in Aurora] for eight years and graduated. But with my depression, then having a kid made it harder."

After living much of her life on the streets, Katrina now understands what the combination of depression and alcohol was doing to her.

"You are happy one minute because you are drinking away your misery, but in the next minute, you know, when you sober up, all that misery is right there … it is up to you to change it."

Katrina is quick to take responsibility and give credit. She worked hard to make this major change in her life, to accept help and get housing. She was so ready. Her son had been taken from her. She was tired; it was not easy working day jobs, anything from shingling roofs to laying down tile.

"I was actually staying on porches. Got a ticket for laying on a church [porch], it was trespassing. Because it was raining, I needed somewhere safe to lay, you know, with all that's going on out there on the streets to a lot of women."

Katrina and Dionshay

No, I do not know what it is like not having a place to get in out of the rain. I am not sure I want to know what's happening to women on the streets.

Katrina proved she could face her issues. Daily Breathalyzer tests and seeing a therapist became her routine. Katrina said, "I started doing everything I had to do."

Today Katrina lives in a Boulder apartment. She dreams of learning about radiology or culinary arts, maybe even auto mechanics. She plans to go to Gateway Community College next fall and is grateful to the Carriage House Community Table, Mental Health Services and Boulder Shelter for the Homeless.

Katrina is determined to break the cycle, not to do to her son what was done to her. "It made me a stronger person, but he deserves a better life." Equally important is her choice to surround herself with the right people. "You can choose the right people to hang around with or you can choose the negative people to hang around with."

Now she shares what she has. Katrina takes food to the homeless and lets them shower in her apartment. When they ask, "How did you do it, Katrina?" she tells them not to be afraid to ask for help, to find one special person to trust.

Katrina asks those with homes to recognize this: "A lot turn up their noses at homeless people. We're not bad people. We may come off as ragged and dirty … a little handout is not gonna hurt. We are thankful for whatever you give us."

In her straightforward way, Katrina gently chides, "Just because we're staying on the street doesn't mean we're different. We're just like you."

Katrina does not see herself as courageous. She is pragmatic about letting the past stay in the past. "Don't look back, look forward. Let's move on to a better and brighter future, you know?"

Yes, Katrina, *now* I know.

Katrina is quick to take responsibility and give credit. She worked hard to make this major change in her life.

Ariana and Roland

by Joy Eckstine

Being transgender is challenging enough; add being homeless and it can be tragic and scary.

Ariana was told when her son Roland was 9 years old that she had to leave her home and would not be allowed to return until she learned to "look and act like a man." Lisa, Roland's other mother, was furious about Ariana's transition to becoming a woman.

Roland described his feelings about Ariana's departure very clearly. "I was sad and resentful, and I blamed myself. I had always felt most understood by Ariana. She supported my creativity." Roland struggled in high school and with the rules in Lisa's home. He joined bands, wrote music and finally one night he broke curfew while recording at a studio. At 17, eight years after Ariana left, he was asked to leave, too.

Ariana has information technology skills and was able to find work at times but experienced economic discrimination on many levels due to being transgendered. She lost a job in 2000 when she was not allowed to pass the United States/Canada border. Her formal identification gave her birth name rather than her chosen name, Ariana.

She became more and more despairing, and turned to alcohol as a way to numb herself. One morning she woke up on the sidewalk in Denver, beaten, robbed and

> Being transgender is challenging enough; add being homeless and it can be tragic and scary.

raped. Ariana described how she at times had found protectors on the street but that the price was always quite high. "Women sleeping alone on the street are very likely to be raped but a trans person sleeping alone on the street is likely to be raped and beaten or even killed," she said.

She said she was told that if she came to Boulder, "People will love you and take care of you." Desperate for safety, she did.

Meanwhile Roland, having been sent away by Lisa, moved to Washington State and became engaged. When his fiancée broke things off in May 2011, he called Ariana, fearing that he, too, might become homeless. With images of her past swirling in her head, she immediately traveled to Washington, fearing that Roland didn't have the skills to keep himself safe on the streets alone. She described that past; being brutally raped five times and "the beatings afterwards were because of the hatred." She spoke calmly but the urgency of protecting Roland was quite real. They described how almost all his possessions have been stolen, and the pain of discovering that his creative work was taken too.

Ariana and Roland describe their relationship: "We want to be together. We care about each other and we encourage each other. Together we are safer and we can be real, no games or pretense." They both describe how difficult it is to trust on the street, where an approach from another homeless person can mean conversation and assistance, or a hustle and danger.

In September, Roland found a 32-hour-per-week job. His face lights up with a smile. With this job and the work that Ariana thinks she can pick up they are optimistic that they can begin to look for housing.

"He's my son, there's nothing I wouldn't do for him," she said.

"I stick by my mom no matter what people think or do," he said.

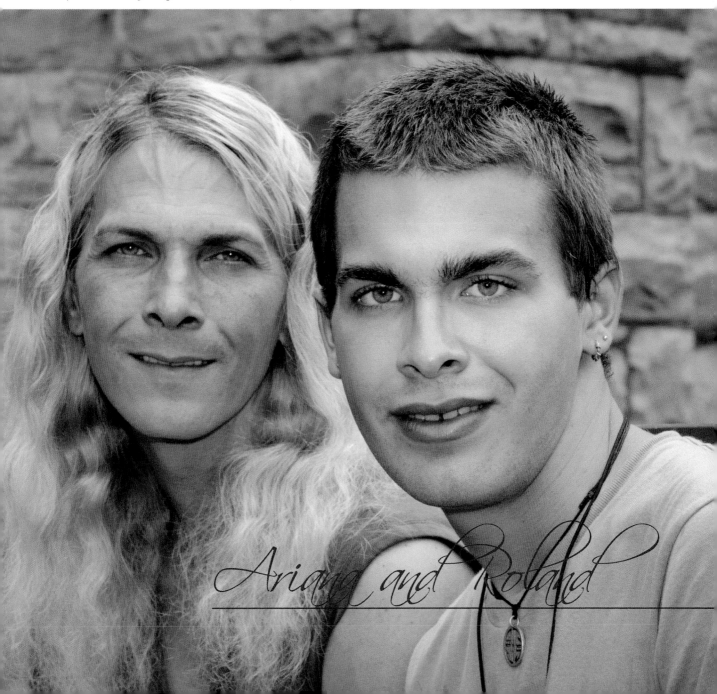

Ariana and Roland

Keith and Angela

Keith and Angela

by Anne Doyle

Angela and her sister hitchhiked to Denver with a truck driver, then hopped the bus to Boulder. At the Boulder Shelter for the Homeless, Angela had a brief conflict with the staff over her desire to watch a Garth Brooks DVD and she sat dejected; Keith couldn't take his eyes off of her. "I noticed her head was down and she was looking all sad. I didn't like to see a person looking sad and I was trying to make a little joke and make her laugh." Angela remembers: "Keith just kept looking at me. Every time I looked up he was staring at me. His smile and his eyes got to me. He does have a beautiful smile and beautiful eyes. And his laugh, of course...Somehow he knew I was a Southern girl."

Keith was right. Angela is from Florida and he is from Texas. It was practically love at first sight. Five months later they were married.

There were no engagement parties, no bridal showers. No gift registries, no bridesmaids. The wedding was simple, held at Angela's mother's place in Arkansas. And so far, there has been no first home. But they are hoping to change that.

Keith has worked all his life and he wants to work now. He moved from Texas to California, where he had a good job but got laid off. He tried to find something else but couldn't, so he came to Colorado. Here he has continued to search for work. While he's

> **Keith has worked all his life and he wants to work now.**

been looking, he gave in and learned a new skill: how to "fly a sign." Standing on the street corner, Keith waits for people driving by to read his message and give him money. He said he hates it. "I was embarrassed. I had always hustled to find something like mowing lawns or moving furniture when I didn't have a permanent job. I made more money doing odd jobs than I do flying a sign." Angela agrees: "It's very stressful to fly a sign."

"Stress" was the first reaction of both Angela and Keith when asked about being homeless. While stress is just a fact of life for most people, those with homes can take a break, step out of the world for a time. For Angela and Keith there is no relief. No place to just be. There is no place to go to be together, alone.

At the Boulder Shelter for the Homeless they can't spend time near one another without being watched to make sure they don't hold hands or hug or kiss. Couples are forbidden to touch, even newlyweds. They must sleep in separate areas: upstairs for the women, downstairs for the men. Not being able to be demonstrative is one source of stress for all homeless couples, Angela said. The frustration with separation then turns into frustration with one another so "there are lots of arguments about childish stuff." Sometimes they use their money to get a motel room away from the crowd in the shelter

Keith and Angela

and beyond the scrutiny of observers.

"Stress and lots of moving around make it difficult," Keith said. "I've been homeless for a year now and I'm trying to get a place to work and improve my life. I'm trying to go to school. I can't do that being homeless, living in the Boulder Shelter, because I can't find time to study and can't find time to rest. That's my dream, to go back to school and get an education in computer programming."

And yet it's hard for Angela to think about Keith getting a job and being away from her all day. She has seizures often and fears no one will be around to help her. But she knows that life will be better for them when he has a regular job. She's trying to get a service dog to support her when Keith is away. "I hate being homeless. I've been homeless since I was 18 — now I'm almost 32 — and I can't stand it. Some people say that I chose to be homeless and that's not true," said Angela. She is thinking about what she might do with more education; she hopes to take online courses in criminal justice.

"Lots of homeless have goals," said Keith. "They keep trying and trying but nothing happens. I understand that it don't happen overnight but you want it to happen before you leave this world."

With steady work Angela and Keith could find an apartment and get a car. They talk about the ordinary activities they would enjoy doing: watching sports, cooking, crafts, hiking and barbecuing. Angela has three children from a former marriage living in foster care in another state. She hopes they can all be together. "We want to have our own place when we have children 'cause we don't want our kids to be taken away by the state and I know if we are homeless that's what's going to happen."

Both Angela and Keith are emphatic that once they get a home, they will still remember what it's like to be homeless. And they want to motivate others to work towards their dreams. Angela said, "The most important thing the homeless can do is to look toward the future, not the past." And that's where this newlywed couple is looking: forward, toward home.

The Intersectors

Intersecting in a meaningful way with the invisible world of homelessness changes us. While the homeless receive much-needed help, compassion swells in the Intersectors. The ten stories on the following pages provide insight into a sample of the Intersectors in the Boulder community and speak to their profound motivations.

The Intersectors

Jonathan and Deborah

by Jonathan Davis

My wife and I grew up in the New York area and lived in the city when we first got married. The city is huge, and so is the homeless population. Many of the street people there were quite aggressive. We were still young and naïve and it was painful and scary to see so many people living on the street. But we soon became inured to them and just looked away.

My wife, Deborah, first suggested we volunteer at the Boulder Shelter for the Homeless 10 years ago, soon after we moved here from California. We'd always been active in the community and just felt it was the right thing to do.

We were both anxious that first night. We were self-conscious. What were homeless people really like? Were they aggressive like in New York? We wanted to get everything right.

We started volunteering as servers in the old Boulder Shelter for the Homeless that was a few blocks south of the current facility on North Broadway. The shelter was in a decrepit old motor lodge, something out of the 1950s and falling apart at the seams. It was hard to believe that it housed over 80 people.

Of course it wasn't hard or scary at all. And over the years our relationship with the Boulder Shelter and its diverse and changing group of residents has deepened in ways we never would have expected. No matter how much we put into it, we always seem to get even more out of it. During any given week it's often the only time when we can step outside of our own day-to-day problems and focus entirely on helping someone else.

And that is priceless.

If you've ever worked as a waiter you know first-hand how arrogant and rude the public can be, no matter how respectful and efficient you are. And these are people with cars and homes and enough money to dine out. But rudeness and bad attitudes are never the case at the Boulder Shelter. We serve 160 meals every

Jonathan and Deborah

night and invariably we receive 160 smiles in return from 160 people who aren't accustomed to getting any smiles at all. In 10 years we've never seen a fight, never heard anything worse than an argument. But we hear "thank you" all the time and we accept a lot of compliments for food that we didn't even prepare.

The best things are the tidbits of good news we hear from residents. When someone who's been down on their luck confides that they finally got a job or an apartment it makes our hearts sing. Sometimes we get Christmas cards. Sometimes we get little gifts. I've got a homeless friend who keeps supplying me with little bottles of his secret hot sauce because we once talked about how much we both love barbecue. Sometimes residents get sick or have accidents and it's wonderful to see them get better.

Every season also brings sadness, unfortunately. Many folks just move on down the road looking for better opportunities elsewhere, and we miss them and wish them the best. Sometimes people get sick and it's hard to watch them go downhill. Sometimes people sober up, then fall off the wagon again and we ache because we know how hard they are trying. Sometimes people die, and that's the hardest pain of all. There's nothing we can do.

One night I flew home from a business trip and the flight was very late. It was my night to serve dinner and instead of changing clothes I asked the company limo driver to take me directly to the Boulder Shelter. It was a very cold and windy night and the residents were lined up outside waiting for evening check-in, stamping their feet to keep warm. Just when we pulled in I realized that it wasn't going to look good for me to step out of the warm, comfortable limo in my best suit and wool coat. I almost didn't open the door.

It was just another affirmation that if our roles were reversed, they would be doing the same for me.

But when I stepped out I saw the huge grins on the faces of all the residents that I'd gotten to know. Lots of them were laughing. That night on the serving line I wasn't the only one dishing it out. It was hysterical. I realized then and there that all the nice clothes and fancy limos in the world didn't change the fact that I was back among friends, just trying to serve the spaghetti and meatballs. It was just another affirmation that if our roles were reversed, they would be doing the same for me.

Wendy & Catalina
by Bunny Hender

Wendy and Catalina know a 14-year-old girl who lives with her mother in a shelter to avoid an abusive father. They know a 10-year-old boy who spends the night in his father's car. They know children who stay in motels with their parents, and many children and families who "double up," living with friends or relatives because they do not have the resources to be in permanent housing of their own. It's the job of Wendy and Catalina, as Boulder Valley School District's homeless liaisons, to make sure that children in these situations get a chance to go to school.

Wendy and Catalina work to carry out the federal McKinney-Vento law, whose intention is to remove all barriers to enrollment, attendance and academic success that children and youth who do not have permanent housing might face. The children, even though not out on the streets, are considered homeless because they don't have a "fixed, regular and adequate nighttime residence."

Students are referred to Wendy and Catalina by shelters, food banks, housing and human services, parents and 53 Boulder Valley School District (BVSD) schools. The schools usually waive all required fees for these students but the two women serve as advocates when students need medical assistance or help in classes. They aid the schools in making contact with the parents and help the parents connect with community services.

When students don't have a permanent address, Catalina and Wendy use the school district's address to cut through red tape. They also provide training for McKinney-Vento liaisons at each school, who in turn train all the teachers in their buildings. The training raises awareness about the law as well as what the students may be experiencing.

Approximately 900 McKinney-Vento children currently are enrolled in the Boulder Valley School system. They range from preschool to high school students, with about 30 to 60 of them in every grade. The test scores for the McKinney-Vento students are usually lower than any other group and poor attendance is a problem; some of the kids have missed so much school that it becomes an uncomfortable place for them. On the other hand, for some of the students, school is the safest and most stable part of their day. The status of each child is confidential, so the other students are usually unaware of the "away from school" situations with which the McKinney-Vento kids must cope.

Catalina and Wendy have had their hearts broken by some situations and are filled with pride and happiness by others. There's the girl whose mother died when she was 13, then her father was deported. She lived with various aunts in different areas but was able to keep attending her "school of origin" because of the McKinney-Vento law. Today she has a job and is very close to getting her certified nursing assistant

> For some of the students, school is the safest and most stable part of their day.

Wendy

Catalina

certificate when she graduates from BVSD.

A father living in a tent with his family in Nederland approached Wendy and Catalina about sending his son to school. They explained the system to him and he got a job, which qualified him to move his family into transitional housing in Boulder. His son enrolled in school. Now the father is working, the son is succeeding in the school system and the family has a house.

A 17-year-old boy was living with his unstable mother in an emergency shelter. When his mother moved away, he moved in with his father. The teen's girlfriend got pregnant and then his father was killed. Although he broke up with his girlfriend, he wanted to stay near his baby, but he had no resources and was about to become homeless. A co-worker of Wendy and Catalina's heard them discussing the case, and took the boy in. He attended school for a while, got his GED, started classes at Front Range Community College and got a job. When his baby and her mother moved to

northern Colorado, he followed to be with the baby. He's now working and going to college. He still calls on a regular basis to check in with Catalina and Wendy, the people who helped him make a life for himself.

Some situations are less resolved. A 13-year-old and her 16-year-old brother came up from El Salvador to live with their uncle. After the girl had to go to

Clinica Family Health Services, the uncle decided he didn't want the kids any more. The only place they could find to stay was with her brother's friends and their mother in an unheated trailer. Although the girl continues to go to school, no one knows what's going to happen.

Both Catalina and Wendy say that the hardest part of their job is when a child asks for something that they aren't able to provide. But when they see a student who isn't connected to school finally make a connection and start succeeding, when the kids realize that they have support, the women feel the rewards of their hard work.

by Tina Downey

"I like to say I fell into this line of work!" Ian has a contagious grin. Not one to hesitate, he begins speaking with passion and purpose while buzzing around his large corner office on his sleek-looking wheelchair. Ian exudes strength and will. This is a man with a mission and if you're willing to listen, he'll share it with you.

At 21, a college wrestler, he was in the prime shape of his life when some late-night, alcohol-infused antics left him riding toward earth on the crown (now detached) of a four-story-tall tree. He and some of the other wrestlers liked to play a game of jumping from treetop to roof to treetop. This jump didn't end well. Landing on his back on the fallen trunk, the diameter of your average keg, severed his spinal cord. He recalls having a spiritual experience as he fell, a significant factor in his eventual recovery.

"Well, OK, game over. So God, we're OK, right?" Ian thought as he fell. "Then I just felt such love, and that love was just waiting for me to grab it and I knew then, even while there in the midst of the fall, that I'd recover." His first thoughts after waking up in the hospital were, "I've got to be strong. I don't want to stress out my mom." He was the injured one, his legs useless, and yet his thoughts were about how his condition would affect others. That positive, selfless attitude served him well in his rehabilitating physical therapy, too. He was the star pupil and worked amazingly hard to recover.

When they were ready to discharge him to a nursing home, as he was unable to live independently at that point, he began to see how we, as a society, have a big problem. As we send disabled people to institutions rather than integrating them into the community, we are in effect rendering them homeless.

Society seems to quickly help people who have definable, visible disabilities. We see a person in a wheelchair, we rush to open doors and ask, "What else can I do?" This seemingly compassionate behavior can make a disabled person feel like, "Wow, all these

Ian

people want to help me. I must be helpless. I must need someone to manage my life for me." This is far from the truth. And those with less visible disabilities are often judged wrongly. Just because a handicap is not obvious we may minimize their needs. We know a paraplegic needs a wheelchair, but maybe the other person's "wheelchair" is medication for a mental condition, and without getting to know them we can't possibly know what they need.

That's where Ian, now the executive director of The Center for People with Disabilities in Boulder, comes into the picture. The Center's mission is to come alongside clients who would like to make changes in their lives, including getting off the street and putting homelessness behind them. The staff is there to help the disabled person navigate through the sometimes confusing requirements to qualify for help. They put clients in the driver's seat and focus on helping them achieve their goals. "We don't do things *for* people, but we do things *with* people," Ian said.

The Center helps identify available resources and work with clients on their plans to make changes. It isn't a place for, "Oh, we're so sorry about your life. We're going to do this for you." It's a place where when they are ready to work on their goals, the Center will be their number one supporter.

> **The Center's mission is to come alongside clients who would like to make changes in their lives.**

By giving the clients that control, the Center honors their right to a place of dignity in society. "Integrating the homeless or disabled (and sometimes it's both) strengthens the moral fiber of a community," Ian said. The best possible solution to problems facing the disabled or homeless is when each person lives as independently as possible. He believes that regardless of physical or mental challenges, all have a place in society, but the places may be different, even for individuals with the same issues.

Ian's zest for life pours forth with each word. This man clearly enjoys his work, and is equally passionate about his private life. Last September he married Elizabeth, a Hospice medical social worker. They have no children, yet. With a joyful grin, he describes some of the amazing adaptive equipment available for disabled athletes that allows him to remain active, in some ways more so than before his accident. His service dog, Aslan, a gentle giant German shepherd, is his constant companion and has even joined him in some civil disobedience as he and a growing group of crusaders rally for the rights of the disabled to live in community, not in institutions.

For Ian, it isn't enough to give these people a face. He wants them to have a voice, too.

Anna Maria

by Jonathan Davis

Anna Maria Pirone was born and raised in New York City and is no stranger to all kinds of street life, good and bad. However, unlike many who just insulate themselves against unpleasantness, she felt called to help people in need. She feels strongly that everyone contains basic goodness and that even those who have been dealt a bad hand have a basic will to survive. All they need is an angel to help them on the way.

Anna started volunteering in New York in sixth grade and hasn't stopped since. She has worked with abused women, has been an advocate for kids in the foster care system, has worked with kids and adults with disabilities and now runs Boulder's only support and advocacy group focusing on homeless youth ages 15 to 24.

Anna shrugs off her calling as just something she does. She said matter-of-factly, "I was just born to do this." A businesswoman and certified public accountant by training, she's also a leader and entrepreneur; she has the energy and compassion to fill an enormous gap in Boulder's social services net by providing basic services and mentoring for Boulder's hard-core street kids.

Homeless kids don't come just from homes that are broken. They come from homes that have completely disintegrated due to abuse, violence, alcoholism, drug addiction and neglect. With nowhere else to turn, the street becomes their home and other street kids become their family.

> **Anna realized that homeless kids were falling through the cracks in Boulder's social services net and decided to do something about it.**

They drink and take drugs and they give up hope, live without dreams.

Most kids in their late teens and early twenties are putting the building blocks of their adult identities into place under the care and guidance of parents or other caring adults. But street kids never get a chance to develop into adults. They don't know how to look for jobs and, even when they do land an interview, they don't have alarm clocks, toiletries or showers. Sixteen-year-olds from distant towns attach themselves to other homeless kids who reinforce the hopelessness of each other's situations. Many kids get dragged into court for offenses they don't understand; they have no identification. They end up adding to the permanent adult homeless population, or in jail, or dead.

Anna realized that homeless kids were falling through the cracks in Boulder's social services net and decided to do something about it. She resurrected a defunct chapter of Stand Up For Kids (www.standup-forkids.org) and opened a drop-in center in August 2010. Stand Up for Kids Boulder has received no federal or local government funding. It operates solely on the generosity of small individual donations, corporate sponsors and volunteer support. The center is open five days a week and provides a place for youth who are living on the streets or are at risk to go and relax from the difficulties of street life. Its model is relationship-based.

The center is there to listen and provide support and guidance to help youth with life choices. They also provide for the tangible needs: hot meals, showers, outdoor gear, clothing, personal hygiene products, computer use, medical, mail and laundry services, state IDs, legal assistance, housing, education, vocational development, life skills, counseling and transportation.

Stand Up For Kids' "on the streets" program, established more than 20 years ago, has helped to feed and clothe thousands of homeless and street kids. Volunteers go out into the streets of Boulder several times a week looking for homeless kids. They often come across kids who haven't eaten, showered or slept for days. Volunteers distribute food packs, hygiene products, clothing and camping supplies.

Anna tells the story of a pregnant homeless teenager who was given a camping ticket for sleeping in a parking garage two days before she gave birth. One of the volunteers was able to find housing for her with a program that shelters pregnant teens.

Anna Maria

Anna has put together a solid business plan and organization that has started making a difference for Boulder's homeless youth, a resource that is able to provide significant levels of social work, advocacy and mentoring. But there is a lot more to do and she and her volunteers work around the clock to raise funds and train more volunteers so they can make an even bigger difference.

It's easy to talk to Anna about her calling but it's hard to confront the enormity of the problem. And it's even harder to confront the fact that our community has neglected the needs of homeless youth.

As Anna says, "Just look around. They are out there." They obviously need and deserve our help. The most hardened street kid has the potential to survive and to dream. And everyone has the potential to be an angel to them.

Cassie

by Michele Weiner-Davis

"You can't judge a book by its cover," Cassie insisted. But in her case, it simply isn't so. As she speaks of her unwavering commitment to social causes and the homeless, it becomes clear that her striking outward beauty is merely a glimpse into the beauty deep inside. Cassie, 21, is a sociology major and political science minor at the University of Colorado and director of the Hunger and Homeless Campaign at the Colorado Public Interest Research Group (CoPIRG). She is passionate about raising awareness of the widespread prejudice regarding homelessness. She is also determined to be an integral part of finding real and lasting solutions to assist this population.

Although Cassie is quick to say that the system is sorely lacking in terms of remedies for homelessness and hunger, she believes political activists such as herself and other students involved in CoPIRG must work within the system to create meaningful change. She inspires students to engage in socially conscious activities, to make a difference in their communities rather than party or participate in other unproductive behaviors. She is wise beyond her years.

CoPIRG is a 30-year-old statewide student organization that tackles issues such as environmental protection, hunger and homelessness. In her role as director of the Hunger and Homelessness Campaign Cassie is charged with the responsibility of enlightening interns about the plight of the homeless and hungry, then bringing their new insights to the student body through community events. She is also committed to teaching students about the discrepancy in food sources available to wealthy and educated populations as compared to those with lower incomes or living at the poverty level both here and abroad. She believes that poverty and hunger are growing global problems. Through raising awareness in the student body and in the community, Cassie hopes to eradicate these problems in the community through public support of

Cassie

fundamental changes to the system.

Cassie seems to take delight in transforming people's perspectives and attitudes about the homeless by offering opportunities to become personally involved with them. For example, when working side-by-side with homeless people to clean up the Boulder Creek path, students learned that, contrary to their beliefs, homeless people are not lazy or unskilled members of society. They have rich stories to tell about their life experiences and the reasons for their homelessness. Students are often surprised that educated, highly successful career people – such as a CEO from a well-known company and a professional concert musician – are not exempt from unemployment and losing their homes. Additionally, she said, "Homeless people are often misunderstood. Many are mentally ill or have brain damage and are sorely in need of services."

Cassie had a personal experience that made her even more committed to eradicating prejudice among CU students. After she served as facilitator at a consciousness-raising event, an anonymous person wrote a letter to a local newspaper calling her a "spoiled brat"

> She is passionate about raising awareness of the widespread prejudice regarding homelessness.

and a "coddled CU student." Cassie is a far cry from either. In addition to being a full-time student, about to graduate from CU and further her education, Cassie volunteers to work with CoPIRG and pays her own way through college with money from part-time employment. Cassie felt judged unfairly, much the way homeless people feel.

Cassie objects to "sticking people in jail" or simply providing shelter and other resources for them, strategies she believes do not get at the root of the problem. She is dedicated to resolving the underlying issues and is a strong believer that "it takes a village." As a society, people need to take care of each other.

Many of Cassie's friends join her in her attempt to change the world. She prefers surrounding herself with people who care about others and tends to shy away from students who are self-absorbed, emotionally detached from society's challenges or judgmental. She contends, "If you aren't pissed off, you aren't paying attention."

Cassie's eyes are wide open and she sees to it that everyone crossing her path is inspired by her vision.

Joy E.
by Jennifer Sleek

Joy has served as the executive director of the Carriage House Community Table since 2005. While her professional training as a licensed clinical social worker and certified addictions counselor equip her to comprehend the complex needs and challenges of the population she serves, her empathy and understanding come from her own traumatic life path. "But for the grace of God, there go I," she said as she recalled the long and difficult journey that led to her tireless commitment to the homeless and marginalized people she serves every day.

Joy grew up in a dysfunctional family system in which she found herself the caretaker for her younger sisters and at times for both of her parents. Her father presented a responsible and respectable persona to the community, she said, but behind closed doors was physically and emotionally abusive to everyone in the family. Joy's mother was emotionally unstable and unable to support and care for herself or her daughters, so Joy became the nurturer and caretaker for her family members, a heavy burden for a young girl.

In this unpredictable and unsafe environment, Joy found solace by escaping into reading, learning and excelling academically in school. She also enjoyed healthy relationships with several stable adults who were positive influences. "My life demonstrates what so many research studies have found – that the presence

> "This is a healing place," she said simply. And it's not only for the people she serves, but for herself as well.

of interested and kind adults can make a profound difference in the life of a child – sometimes the difference between going awry and learning to be strong and resilient," she said. It would have been easy for her to make different choices in her life, but she determined to finish high school and pursue a college education, challenging endeavors given the lack of financial and emotional resources available from her family.

In college Joy participated in a project that would shift her perspective and ultimately, her life course. Along with a group of students, she took part in a "sleep-out" for a week in the freezing month of March to raise money for an area homeless shelter. Having her eyes opened to the harsh realities of life on the street, she worked at a homeless shelter for five years until returning to graduate school to earn her master's degree.

Joy made other major life changes and moved from the east coast to Colorado, married and experienced some tumultuous and difficult personal and relational transitions. After a long, emotional struggle with infertility, her first marriage crumbled. A new marriage and a baby initially brought hope, but unforeseen difficulties surfaced with both, and Joy found herself facing another divorce and the prospect of raising a special needs child on her own. The marriage ended after a lot of relational trauma and a second child.

As Joy became a single mother she realized that

she simply did not have the monetary resources to make it on her own. She became resourceful and reached out for any assistance she could find. Fortunately, because of her background in social work and her position at the Carriage House Community Table, she was aware of agencies and organizations that helped children and mothers. At first as she talked with people who were also colleagues, she had to explain that she was there as someone who needed assistance in order to keep her family clothed, fed and

Joy

sheltered. She was able to piece together a meager existence with resources from these organizations and loans from family and friends. She remembers sleeping on couches in friends' basements and wondering where she would stay the next week. "I had to ask myself, 'What if I didn't have these people in my life to help me? What if I was someone who felt shy about asking for help? Where would I be?'"

Since that low point in her life four years ago, Joy has worked tenaciously to put her life back together and build a better future for herself and her children.

She has chosen to take these painful firsthand experiences and use them to create a fulfilling life for herself, as well as be there for others who find themselves in similar need.

"I've made a lot of mistakes, so I just don't define people by their mistakes," she said. "I get to hear people's stories. I get to be a witness to their resilience. I get to see the extremes of human behavior, which include some rotten behavior at times, but also on a daily basis I see people being generous and kind, grateful and working together. I see that way more than I see anything else. This is an instant antidote to self-pity."

It's clear that Joy's passion for her work at the Carriage House Community Table is deep and personal. She recognizes that it's not about trying to solve others' problems, but rather connecting and being present with them as people. She stopped for a moment, then summed up her beliefs and feelings about the Carriage House Community Table; "This is a healing place," she said simply. And it's not only for the people she serves, but for herself as well.

Anne

by Kristin Pazulski

Anne wasn't always interested in working with the homeless community. For years she worked in health care as a consultant to hospitals, helping them improve the care they provided patients.

But in 2002 she and her husband, after 10 years of consulting together, burned out.

"We went and lived in France for four years," she said. "We got really disgusted with the health care field and so we sold our house, got rid of all our stuff, and we moved to France and said we were never coming back."

But they did come back, moving to Boulder when their daughter wanted to go to high school in the States. Anne brought with her a new outlook on life. While overseas she had developed a new relationship with church and God, and decided she needed to live her life for others.

"I believed in God before, but I hadn't really lived a life that said [it]. … I want to love my neighbor and figure out what I can do to make things better

Anne

for other people because … we all need that."

She believed the homeless most needed help. She wanted to get to know this population in Boulder, misunderstood often through ignorance, and let them know someone was listening.

"I just felt folks in that population didn't have people to pay attention to them. So I thought I would like to be available to them."

She started as a "listener" at the Carriage House Community Table. As a listener, she would do just that. Sitting or standing in the common area of the small day center, she would listen to people's stories, thoughts, hopes and fears. To be a true listener in the way she practices it, she explained, you take away the need to relate to the person. You don't interject your experiences into a conversation. You make yourself "fully present" to that person.

"Sometimes what they would tell me wasn't even true. I don't think they were telling me to lie. To

them it was true right then," she said. "None of that mattered to me. I wasn't in a situation where I had to call them on it or say anything about it. It was always OK."

Along with her work at the Carriage House Community Table, Anne became involved with the Boulder Outreach for Homeless Overflow (BOHO) and in June 2011 was named chair of the board. But still, she had more to give.

Last March, Boulder Medical Respite emerged from her efforts. Collaborating with various institutions, including Boulder Community Hospital, Boulder Shelter for the Homeless, the Carriage House Community Table, Boulder's Clinica Family Health Services and BOHO, Anne is voluntarily (for now) directing the new respite program, which offers a motel room to homeless persons recuperating from injuries, hospital stays and illness.

"Oftentimes when people get sick or have an injury, they don't have any place to go to just get better," she said. "So [there's a gap] if you're not sick enough to be in the hospital, but you're too sick to be doing your daily activities out on the street. That's why we decided we needed respite care." To ensure that the most critical needs are met, clients are identified by Clinica Family Health Services and Boulder Community Hospital. Anne, along with volunteer nurses who care for the medical

> Sitting or standing in the common area of the small day center, she would listen to people's stories, thoughts, hopes and fears.

side of things, visits each of the patients in the program daily, bringing boxes of food, a listening ear and any help she can.

The program participants are truly grateful. "Every angle that I needed was taken care of … it's a good thing for people emotionally, physically, even spiritually."

Anne recognizes that as the program grows, she can't keep visiting every person daily. Currently in a pilot phase, it served eight people from March through July 2011. Summer is slower for a respite program, she said, since it's easier to stay on the streets in the warmer weather. As colder weather hits, she expects that the clientele will increase. She plans to coordinate a corps of volunteers, each of whom will care for one person. No matter the illness, the needs or the wants, the volunteer will visit daily, listen and help.

The program's launch has been funded by organizational and individual donations but is working to discover a regular funding source. At that point Anne wants the program to bring in as many persons as possible.

She has bigger dreams for the future. "I keep having this image of a house, where you have four or five bedrooms, and somebody lives in the house," she said, seeing it clearly in her mind. "So when somebody needs to come home for home care, they literally come into that house and stay."

Joe

by Andrea Binder

"During the winter months I go out one night each week to help find the homeless and get them into a warming center," Joe said. He has been retired for the past eight years and loves to ski. But his love for his work with the homeless population far exceeds his love of sports or his retirement hobbies. You might say that Joe's heart's desire is helping the homeless, keeping people from freezing.

More than 20 years ago Joe began his work with the homeless in Washington, D.C., simply by feeding them. "That's when I learned how important it is to ask, 'What is your name?'" It was also a pivotal point in Joe's life, where he clearly focused on some very important truths: Homeless people are real people with given names, a past childhood, a present hope and a future dream to have a home.

Joe takes his dog, Cody, out to visit the men and women living on the street. Their need for physical touch and affection is apparent as Cody gives sloppy wet kisses to each one. In return, they express love and affection freely and incautiously to the dog. This is a beautiful reminder of what affection without bias can look like. Clearly wanting to educate, Joe said, "No one is homeless by choice or wants to be homeless."

Being homeless is hard work, he said. On any typical day a homeless person will walk three to 10 miles just to find basic survival needs like food, medical attention or shelter. Having a safe place to sleep each night is elusive. Sleep deprivation is a constant companion. All experience physical trauma and it is common for homeless women to be raped. No wonder the life span of a homeless person is 40 to 50 years.

Things other people take for granted, like waking up in a warm, comfortable bed at midnight to use the bathroom, take all of a homeless person's mental and physical energies to sort out, Joe said. Where will I get my next meal? How safe is it to be here? Where should I sleep? What if I need to use the toilet in the middle of the night, where will I go?

It really gets down to basics, he said. Homeless people feel invisible. Helping the homeless begins with understanding in the heart that they are real people. They don't just need or want a handout. Eye contact, a smile and a "hello" go a long way to reassure homeless people that you see them.

According to Joe, Boulder County does a good job helping the homeless, yet there is always a need for more. He believes that merely having all the services for the homeless in close proximity would ease their burden. He dreams about a housing-first program in Boulder that would use empty buildings to create homes for the homeless.

His mission is evident; he wants to enlighten everyone about this issue that tugs so strongly at his

> Homeless people are real people with given names, a past childhood, a present hope and a future dream to have a home.

heart. "Most people who are homeless in Boulder County are actually from Boulder," he said. "It is a myth that Boulder is a magnet for the homeless [from other places]." "These are our own citizens" who have fallen on hard times, are struggling with an early life of trauma or mental or physical illnesses.

What keeps Joe going? "Working with the homeless feels good. It gets me out of my box. I get to meet wonderful people," he said. "It is priceless, rewarding and gives me a deep appreciation for what I have." Joe strives to demonstrate the importance of being a caring and observant community. "We have to offer help, do more and remember that a homeless person is a real person." He sees people looking through or overtly past a homeless man or woman. He believes that simply bestowing the dignity and respect of acknowledgement affects a homeless person in a profound way.

Breaking the myths, stereotypes and faulty beliefs about why a homeless person is homeless is key to helping. And helping, according to Joe, doesn't have to be a big commitment of time or resources. Helping can be as simple as making an authentic connection with a homeless person: Smile, look them in the eye and ask, "What's your name?"

What would it do to our hearts if we tried that today? In Boulder County, 1,050 homeless people were

Joe

counted on January 27, 2009. 73 percent cited Boulder County as their last permanent county of residence

2009 PIT - Metropolitan Denver Homeless Initiative (MDHI).

Betsy

by Doug Hill

Thirty-two years ago Betsy walked into Boulder's People's Clinic for its pregnancy prenatal services. Today, she is its clinical nurse specialist/homeless outreach nurse.

Betsy joined the clinic in 2004 shortly after returning from 18 months of providing care in rural Nicaragua, a role she has repeated on subsequent trips. In translating her Central American experiences to stateside community health, she has found "similar frustrations to both ... in kinds of work and in trying to move things just an inch ... in the lack of resources, lack of money, knowledge deficits."

Boulder, known for land preservation, a broad range of spiritual beliefs, excellent public services and concern for both humankind and wild animalkind, is also home to a top-notch community health center, Clinica Family Health Services/People's Clinic Site.

The downtown nonprofit clinic's mission is to serve the uninsured and the underinsured. But Betsy said many also continue to use the clinic even after obtaining well-paid work and quality health insurance. "We probably have services available you wouldn't even dream of getting in a private doctor's office: mental health professionals, case managers, nutritionists. People's health is more than just the physical."

Three years ago Betsy took on the job of homeless outreach nurse along with her other duties. But after a year the need for a nurse dedicated entirely to the growing homeless population became clear. Today the majority of Betsy's time is spent off-site, away from Clinica itself. She spends regular hours at the Boulder Shelter for the Homeless, the Carriage House Community Table, Attention Homes, Stand-Up for Kids and Echo House, among others. Betsy sees education as a vital part of her work, providing information during every interaction with a patient. "Whether it's quitting smoking or better skin care or substance use ... generally there's some education component I'm trying to bring into it."

Betsy

Navigating the medical system is difficult for everyone: communication, sharing information, follow-up care, claims. Now add the dimension of trauma — physical, emotional, economic, substance abuse – that is statistically characteristic of the homeless life. Betsy recognizes that her patients have suffered trouble in their lives and she strives to come from a place of compassion.

"I get upset at the medical system. I've been a nurse for going on 30 years and ... we don't make it easy for people to interact with the medical system. For most people it's really a difficult experience, especially when they're challenged in making their way through their daily lives. I feel like the medical system isn't user-friendly and that's frustrating to me. I work hard to change it." That requires flexibility, creativity and tenacity. "I'll schedule myself an appointment with somebody, with their doctor, if they're feeling uncomfortable or don't feel like they can get their needs across."

A key turning point in the clinic's ability to provide off-site care to the homeless was its adoption of electronic medical records. That choice made Betsy's position far more effective and brought the homeless closer. Information can be shared and follow-up care is now attainable.

Though her work is naturally draining, she stressed that it's ultimately rewarding. "People are so thankful to get care on their own turf ... even when I don't feel like I'm doing a whole lot to change up their circumstances. It's hard to beat that in your work life."

Betsy identifies housing as the number one problem

> **Our grant is $100,000 and last year we provided $900,000 worth of care to the homeless population.**

in her work. "It's just extremely difficult for people with chronic health conditions to live on the street," she said. Medications need refrigeration. A healthy diet demands a kitchen. Sickness requires bed rest. And the homeless population is growing sicker: diabetes, cancer, hypertension. Some particularly difficult treatments, including those for Hepatitis-C and tuberculosis, can't even *begin* until a patient is adequately housed. "We need supportive housing."

The average age of death of a homeless person in Boulder? Forty-seven.

From 2008 to 2009, the number of homeless people under *Clinica's* care nearly doubled. Currently, 17 percent of its patients are homeless. The staff works hard to care for every one of them, stretching its budget to do the impossible. "The clinic supports people tremendously in terms of health care. Our grant is $100,000 and last year we provided $900,000 worth of care to the homeless population."

Betsy can go home but her work rarely stays at work, especially on cold nights or holidays. "It's hard to know this many people in crisis all the time. It's so outside the realm of most people's daily life that it's hard to share it sometimes."

But she presses on. "We can't ignore that people are here. And if we don't provide health care in a cohesive manner, it's going to happen in the emergency room and that's not the right place for people to be taken care of. They're not going to go away just because we pretend they're not here. It could be any of us trying to connect in those circumstances."

The Intersectors

Rabbi Bronstein

by Lisa Trank

As a parent eager to teach important values to my children, I see homelessness through the eyes of my three daughters. We've donated clothing, helped with food drives and organized Thanksgiving meals. But one night two winters ago we encountered a stranger who shifted and deepened our awareness and gave a real face to homelessness.

It was the first night of Chanukah and we'd stopped at a store to buy wine for our dinner hosts. Waiting in the car I saw her. Looking about 75 years old and wearing a light blue parka she held a neatly written sign: "Disabled. Homeless. Gas. Food. Money." She had a walker and an oxygen tank next to her. I sighed deeply and caught the girls' attention.

I unlocked the door and got out. "Mama, what are you doing?"

"I'm giving the lady some latkes." I tried to approach with respect. She looked up at me as I offered her the foil-wrapped package. "It's just some potato pancakes, and here's five dollars."

She smiled. "Thanks, I love potato pancakes."

"Please tell me you have somewhere warm to sleep tonight." The temperatures in Colorado had been below zero for the past two weeks. She assured me she'd called her sister. She thanked me and I wished her well.

This experience has stayed with me and I took the opportunity of this interview to better understand what my religious tradition of Judaism taught regarding the homeless. Rabbi Deborah Bronstein, of Boulder's Congregation Har HaShem, has been an active advocate for the homeless throughout her rabbinical career. For the past two years, the synagogue and a number of churches in Boulder have participated in BOHO, Boulder Outreach for Homeless Overflow. During the cold winter months these faith communities invite homeless people to stay as their guests in a safe environment.

As we sat in her office, I asked Rabbi Bronstein what the Jewish responsibility is to homelessness: "We are all supposed to respond," Rabbi Bronstein answered. "We need to respond to the immediate problem and then there is the more structured response ... which requires us to provide adequate housing. Intrinsic to Judaism is that the world belongs to God and we're renters. ... If everything belongs to God, then there is a fee — feeding the poor, housing the homeless — that is our rent. The Torah tells us "The edges of the [farm] field don't belong to us, they belong to the people who are in need, the widows, orphans or the stranger. Anything you drop or forget or leave behind, everything you miss [during the harvest], doesn't belong to you anymore. We're all created in the image of God – righteousness demands that we help each other."

Rabbi Bronstein brought a remarkable insight to

> If you have nothing to give, you can still give eye contact and a hello. Acknowledge the other person's dignity and humanity.

the Jewish connection to homelessness as it relates to the story of Passover. "The whole experience of the Seder (the meal in which the story of the Jews' exodus from Egypt is told) is where we remember we were slaves and persecuted, and then wanderers, homeless, in the wilderness." She spoke of a section of the Torah where one mitzvah, a good deed, is repeated 36 times: Don't oppress the stranger, make sure you take care of the stranger, whoever the stranger is."

Rabbi Bronstein emphasized that while a congregation or church

Rabbi Deborah Bronstein

allows us to work through a larger organization, one person can make a difference. She shared the story of a young woman in her congregation who was concerned about homelessness. She noticed how many lunches were going untouched at her school. She was also acutely aware of how many of her fellow students didn't have lunch. She made an arrangement with the vice principal to leave uneaten food for those who needed lunch. From one proactive act of kindness, the initiative grew as she asked other middle schools to participate.

Rabbi Bronstein talked about the courage of the

homeless and our responsibility to reach out. "If you have nothing to give, you can still give eye contact and a hello. Acknowledge the other person's dignity and humanity. There is so much tragedy in people dying for stupid reasons — cold, violence. ... As Jews, we're commanded to not stand idly by; we're commanded to take care of each other."

Shabbat, the Jewish Sabbath, was coming near and we finished our late afternoon conversation.

My mind drifted back to that frigid night two years ago. Getting back in the car with my girls as witnesses, I called the Boulder Shelter for the Homeless to try to figure out how to get the woman to a warm place for the night. It was suggested I call the police and see if they'd come and get her without making her feel like a criminal. When I described the older woman's situation and location, the police dispatcher promised to send a car.

Rabbi Bronstein's words stay with me: Please don't oppress the stranger. Make sure you take care of the stranger, whoever that stranger may be.

What can you do?

The problem of homelessness can seem daunting and overwhelming. The thought of talking to a stranger huddled on a park bench can be scary and uncomfortable. "Love thy neighbor as thyself." Nice thought, but how do you do it?

Small acts mean a great deal as articulated by the people in this book. Here are a few small ideas that will be well received by the homeless population:

1. Smile and make eye contact with people on the streets. This bestows dignity and humanity, an inexpensive yet powerful gift. The "hello" greeting by the Zulu in South Africa is "Sawubona" which means, "I see you." That's the point.

2. Go downtown with a friend or friends (we don't recommend doing this alone). Buy cups of coffee or a bag of take-out food. Find a homeless person and share your gifts and enjoy a conversation. No agenda, no plans, no purpose other than to be with that person.

3. Is it cold outside? Go to your closet and grab the sweater, sweatshirt, pair of gloves or coat you haven't worn in years. Call up several friends and tell them to do the same. Hand out your warm clothing to the men or women huddled under the overpass or in a doorway.

4. Have something readily on hand to share with someone "flying a sign" or asking for a handout: a pair of new, thick socks (appreciated even in the warm months), bottled water, granola bars, a bus pass, or a gift certificate to a local grocery store or fast-food restaurant.

5. Purchase and give away vouchers from the Bridge House's Boulder Change program (in person or on-line), that can be redeemed at nearly 20 local vendors including: King Soopers, the RTD bus station, some Conoco gas stations, Boulder recreation centers, the Mental Health Center and a number of restaurants. The vouchers may not be used for alcohol or tobacco products and no cash change is returned to the user.

6. Volunteer at one of the many service organizations mentioned in this book. Show up early and/or stay late to have conversations with the people you're serving.

The Writing Team

Lori Batcheller is a Boulder-based freelance writer and massage/yoga therapist specializing in health, disabilities, yoga and inspirational profiles. She writes for magazines, web-

sites and journals including www.disaboom.com and Kripalu Center for Yoga & Health. Her books include *Alpine Achievement: A Chronicle of the United States Disabled Ski Team*. www.lbcreative.com.

Andrea Binder has shared her own healing journey around the world as a speaker, counselor and author. She is the mother of two amaz-

ing adult children and four beautiful grandchildren. She is joyfully married to her husband of 36 years. Together, they love to travel.

Constance E. Boyle (MFA, Goddard 1994) writes prose and poetry. Journal publications include *Sliver of Stone*, *Melusine*, and poems forthcoming in *poemmemoirstory*. Her chapbook, *Double*

Exposure, placed first in the 2005 Plan B Press Poetry Competition. Connie was an adolescent medical provider (PA) at Denver Health for 28 years.

Ann Brandt's last book *A Caregiver's Story: Coping with a Loved One's Life-Threatening Illness* includes information on surviving cancer, based on personal experience caring for her husband. Visit her at

www.annkbrandt.com and click on her blog, "Another Point of View."

Hollis Brooks, a Boulder-based freelance writer, specializes in stories about people, travel, restaurants and trends. A former New Yorker, Brooks was a longtime editor at *Skiing* magazine, and a contributing editor at InStyle

magazine. She's a corporate event planner organizing gatherings for the creative divisions at Apple and Adobe.

Jodi Burnett is a new author from Broomfield, Colorado. She is "Mom" to four amazing people, "Grammie" to three beautiful cherubs, and has been married to the love of her life for 28 years. Jodi is looking forward to her next

project, an historical fiction based in Scotland and Germany.

Eliza Cross is an award-winning writer and the author of five books. Her articles have appeared in numerous publications, including *Parents, Writers' Digest, Natural Home,* and *Mountain Living*. She writes about simplicity,

organic gardening, good food and personal finance at HappySimpleLiving.com, and lives with her family in Denver.

Tina Downey, born in Sweden, now calls Colorado home. Her engineer-inventor husband and two active teenage boys keep life from ever being dull. She enjoys the outdoors, cooking, reading and knitting. Her blog, "Life

is Good" feeds her need to write daily, and she's working on her first novel.

Anne Doyle enjoyed a successful health care career, then shucked job and possessions to move her family to France, where she was called to "love your neighbor." She returned to Boulder and fulfills that call by building community between those with and without homes, through BOHO and Medical Respite Boulder.

Joy Eckstine, Executive Director, the Carriage House Community Table, has spent her professional life working with challenging populations: the severely mentally ill, dual-diagnosed prisoners, ex-prisoners and the homeless.

She's received Boulder County's Victim Advocacy Award, the Group Publishing Outstanding Nonprofit in Northern Colorado, and Boulder County Social Worker of the Year.

Deborah Fryer is a documentary filmmaker and freelance writer. She has worked for *PBS, Frontline, Nova, Discovery, The History Channel,* and *MSNBC,* as well as for numerous non-profits creating educational videos. Deborah is drawn to stories about health, the

environment and the mind-body connection. Please visit www.lilafilms.com for more information.

Carol Grever has been a writer, businesswoman, English professor and philanthropist. From personal experience, she has written two books and produced a documentary on straight spouse recovery. A recognized

spokesperson on mixed-orientation marriages, she's appeared on major network TV shows, including *The Oprah Winfrey Show, Anderson Cooper,* and *Good Morning America*.

Kate Guilford grew up in a small, South Georgia town when all blackberries were eaten and no one had heard of Google or apps. A move west after college transformed her into a Colorado woman. After a colorful patchwork quilt of careers, Hakomi therapy and freelance writing won her heart.

Doug Hill has worked as an industrial arts teacher, a barista, a coffin builder, a painter, a cabinetmaker, and a videographer. His two months' homeless in Boulder was one of his greatest learning experiences second only to volunteering in tsunami-affected Thailand. Doug currently lives in a tipi outside Crestone, CO.

Cheri Hoffer is a freelance writer living in the mountains near Lyons, Colorado. She shares her home with many great dogs that she boards while her clients travel, and the dogs never complain about the quality of a first draft.

Tim Johnson continues to mediate an ongoing argument in his brain by pursuing writing, photography, music and occasionally technology, and extends profound apologies to whichever of these pursuits you've been subjected most recently.

Kathy Kaiser is a free-lance writer and editor based in Boulder, Colorado. A long-time resident of Boulder, she worked for a variety of publications before starting her own business. She can be contacted at www.kathykaiser.net.

Mary Beth Lagerborg has written nine non-fiction books, including *Once-a-Month Cooking*, which has sold more than 500,000 copies. Currently she is writing people's memoirs or family or organizational histories as a personal historian, and completing a first novel set in Grand Lake, Colorado, in 1947. She lives in Littleton, Colorado

Curtine Metcalf, poet, freelance writer of human interest non-fiction, writes regionally and is contributing to the upcoming book, *Unraveling Mysteries: An Anthology of Women and Aging*, edited by Jyoti Wind. A passionate  volunteer, animal and child activist and 'humanitarian,' she believes history and stories need to be shared.

Sharon Monroe is the founder and director of the Colorado Writers Workshop in Boulder, Colorado. She studied in an out-of residency MFA of Creative Writing program offered by author Pam Houston, University of  California, Davis. She writes novels, short stories and inspirational articles. Sharon and her husband, Mark, live in Louisville.

Maryjo Faith Morgan (Mj-Morgan.com) is a full time writer with hundreds of published articles. She seeks to encourage and enlighten her readers with her subjects' creativity or business acumen. Bios and case studies are her  favorite assignments. A partner in FredsUsedWebsites.com, she loves riding her tandem with husband Fred Richart.

Elle Page consults in communication, team health and helping leaders and their organizations become more effective. She is also an executive coach enhancing executives' professional effectiveness and personal  satisfaction. She loves to bring beauty, order and simplicity to her work, home, garden and words.

Taylor Pappas is a student at the University of Colorado at Boulder studying International Affairs. Raised in Colorado, Taylor has a great appreciation for the outdoors and the community of Boulder. In his free time,  Taylor enjoys spending time with his wonderful family, friends and his five dogs.

Kristin Pazulski started as a reporter in Philadelphia before venturing to Los Angeles and finally to Denver. Finding her passion in helping people as well as writing, she began writing for the *Denver VOICE*, and recently took over management and fundraising for the street paper.

Marsha J. Perlman's early years in New York City influenced her careers in education and photojournalism. Her poetry, prose and photos, reflecting a love of outdoor life in Colorado and Florida, appear in books, magazines,  journals and online. In *Spirit Life*, she invites the reader to enjoy and protect our fragile environment.

Jennifer Sleek returned to graduate school after 20 years in the field of corporate communications, earned a master's degree in professional counseling, and is now a practicing psychotherapist. She and husband Stein  Klevdal have been married for 25 years and are the proud parents of daughter Jordan and son Christian.

Lisa Trank lives in Longmont, Colorado, with her family. She holds an MFA in Writing and Poetics from Naropa University and her work has appeared in the University of Denver magazine, Salon.com, the Longmont Ledger, the Arts Paper and Bombay Gin.

Mandy Walker believes that stories have the power to change the world, opening us up to new possibilities and compassion for our fellow beings. Her website, www.SinceMyDivorce.com is a collection of interviews with  women about life after the end of marriage: the pains, the obstacles, the triumphs and joys.

Michele Weiner-Davis, MSW is a relationship expert, best-selling author, speaker, director of The Divorce Busting® Center in Boulder, Colorado, and Founder of www.divorcebusting.com. Her work is highly regarded and  she has received several professional awards, and has been featured in countless newspapers, magazines and national television and radio shows.

Craig Yager is a Boulder boy who, before his retirement taught in Boulder Valley since 1974. He is a singer/songwriter with twelve of his musicals for young people produced in Boulder schools. He's presently working on a  novel about Boulder in the 1930's, plus several short stories and nonfiction pieces.

Susan Deans is a freelance writer and editor, retired after 30 years in the newspaper business. Most recently she was editor and vice president of the *Daily Camera* in Boulder. She began her journalism career as a reporter at the *Camera* in 1977 after earning a master's degree in journalism from the University of Colorado. She has a bachelor's degree in English from Knox College, Galesburg, Illinois. In fall 2007, after leaving the *Camera*, she taught journalism as a visiting professor at Knox.

She serves on the boards of the City of Boulder's Downtown Management Commission, the Imagine! Foundation and the Dairy Center for the Arts. She also has served on the Knox College Board of Trustees and on the boards of the Boulder Rotary Club, Boulder History Museum and Historic Boulder.

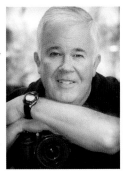

David M. Page has been a photographer ever since exploring f-stops and shutter speeds in junior high school in the late 1960s. He sold his first journalistic photo before entering high school and won his first photographic awards in college.

Bachelor's and Master's degrees in Business Administration opened the world of management to him and David built a career in the corporate world. Today, in addition to his wedding, portrait and fine art photography through DMPage Images, David is a consultant to management and leadership via his consulting practice, Engage Leadership, Inc.

Addtional writers for whom bios were not available:

Jonathan Davis

Tom deMers

Bunny Hender

Jerrie Hurd

Terri Sternberg

The Rotary Club of Niwot is a dynamic group of professionals devoted to serving both the local and international communities. We meet weekly to support projects that promote the common good, and have fun doing it.

The Club uses all fundraising monies for service projects in our local community as well as participating in projects around the world. We are pleased to be a major sponsor of *Until They Have Faces*.

We meet each Thursday morning at the Left Hand Grange in Niwot at 7:15 am.

International Baccalaureate Diploma Programme Niwot High School, Niwot, Colorado

The International Baccalaureate (IB) Diploma Programme, housed at Niwot High School is a rigorous course of study designed to meet the academic needs of highly motivated secondary students and to promote international mindedness. Founded in Europe in 1968, the IB has expanded to thousands of schools worldwide. Niwot High School's IB Diploma Programme, authorized in 2001, is the only one in the St. Vrain Valley School District.

The effectiveness of the IB Diploma Programme is due to the comprehensive nature of the program. IB Diploma Programme requires each student to take rigorous courses in six academic areas that culminate in a college-level examination in each subject. They are also required to complete core components that include critical thinking, creativity, action, service and a college-level research essay. Many IB Diploma candidates enter college at the sophomore level due to state legislation supporting IB. About one third of the Niwot High School student body is enrolled in the Niwot Pre-IB (9th & 10th) and IB Diploma Programme (11th & 12th).

The IB Diploma Programme is highly recognized by universities throughout the world, and IB is considered the most rigorous and distinguished high school program available. Informational meetings for students interested in enrolling in IB at Niwot High School are held in November and December each year, with applications due before Christmas break. Late applications may also be considered. Anyone with questions about IB may call the Niwot High School IB office at 303-652-2550. Additional information about Niwot's IB Programme may be found at nhs.stvrain.k12.co.us.

International Baccalaureate Programme information may be found at www.ibo.org.

DMPage Images supports many local projects. Much of this support comes through donating products and services to the causes and silent auctions of non-profit organizations that strive to make our community a better and more enjoyable place in which to live. We are delighted to have contributed time and expertise in capturing the portraits of *Until They Have Faces*. We are also pleased to donate to this project's success and to the needs of BOHO and the Carriage House Community Table.

Wedding, Portrait & Fine Art Photography
www.DMPageImages.com
303.652.9975

Professional Photographers
of America

Boulder Valley Rotary Club

Service above self is a commitment that defines Rotarians as a whole and lives pure and true within the Boulder Valley Rotary Club (BVRC). Through the avenue of community service within the club, the BVRC selects focus areas to help ensure the greatest coordinated community impact. In the recent years we have included hunger and homelessness in our community among our top focus areas.

We are honored to support this effort initiated within the Rotary Club of Niwot to raise awareness of homelessness in the Boulder area and to support key agency leaders. The BVRC feels a kindred spirit with the Niwot Rotary in facing this issue head on with compassion, volunteerism, and financial support. Over the years there has been a natural connection with this issue and the Boulder Valley Rotary Club.

Now in our 21st year, our very successful BVRC coat drive generates thousands of coats each year in partnership with the Boulder Valley School District and with the benevolent support of Art Cleaners, which dry-cleans every coat. These coats are distributed each year by club members to many in need within the Boulder community.

Other support from the BVRC has included renovation work at BCATH (Boulder County Assisted Transitional Housing), volunteer and contribution efforts to EFFA (Emergency Family Assistance Association), Community Food Share, Boulder Shelter for the Homeless, Carriage House, Lamb's Lunch and hundreds of volunteer hours from the members.

The Boulder Valley Rotary Club is a vibrant group that shares lunch each Tuesday at The Spice of Life, with engaging speakers and a true camaraderie felt by all who participate.

Project Revive is a city transformation initiative to create common ground in order to serve the common good. It is a long-term macro project designed to advance the ideals of appreciation, inspiration, innovation, education and collaboration and is composed of many micro projects such as the production of this book and the creek cleanup event that inspired it.

We infuse financial and social capital into innovative ideas to create tipping points for dreams that might otherwise lay dormant in the minds of social change entrepreneurs. The medical respite program that Anne shares in her story is another example of an idea we helped make a reality.

The title of this project was loosely inspired by the C.S. Lewis novel '*Till We Have Faces*, a reinterpretation of the classic mythological story of Cupid and Psyche. All three of these stories raise probing questions about the meaning of beauty, identity, love, isolation, and longing.

Most people encounter the homeless as nameless, faceless, caricatures. Our fears and prejudices predispose us to experience them detached from their dignity and individuality. For me, the essence of creating common ground in this context is to give voice to their stories and visibility to their faces. I am grateful to David and Elle for serving the common good by blessing us with both.

Ken Miller

Director, Project Revive

Urban Mattress is committed to the community and honored to be a part of this project which focuses on lending respect to all the people in our city. We are a locally owned and operated family business that seeks to provide the best service, prices and products available while supporting the community at large. We are proud to contribute a percentage of our store sales to the work of Project Revive and support many charities including the Carriage House Community Table. Customers have the option to support local charities with their purchase.

We also take our responsibility for protecting the environment very seriously by offering eco-friendly products that use renewable resources, are bio-degradable, and eliminate chemical off-gassing.

Urban Mattress offers the most competitive pricing for mattresses, pillows and accessories. We buy our products at the same price as the large chain stores and pass those savings on to you. Because we are local your tax dollars stay right here to benefit your community.

Research shows that most peoples' health increases greatly by upgrading their mattress and increasing their deep sleep. Our products are the newest and most technologically advanced sleeping systems on the market. We are sleep experts and enjoy helping you choose the right mattress for you.

Our goal is simple — to continually grow our business by consistently doing the right thing and in the process help to make our customers our greatest fans.

The Community Foundation Serving Boulder County is the place for inspired giving. It was founded in 1991 to encourage philanthropy and create opportunities to improve the quality of life in Boulder County, and has granted more than $43 million to non-profit groups since then. The Foundation's staff offer personal service for donors with endowment funds. Donors may also give to our unrestricted grant-making fund, The Community Trust, which allows us to accomplish outcomes in partnership with our donors that cannot be achieved alone.

The Community Foundation is also the place for positive community change. We help strengthen non-profit groups by helping them to identify needs and build capacity. We compile and publish Boulder County TRENDS, a community indicators report. This

The Community Foundation
BOULDER COUNTY

resource guide assists local health care, education, arts, environmental, and business leaders in gauging areas where we are currently excelling and where we need to focus further attention.

We take this community leadership role quite seriously, knowing that often issues are left for "someone else to tackle." When no one else comes forward, The Community Foundation steps in, convening the key players and stakeholders to move forward toward solutions. For more on our Civic Engagement and the Foundation, please visit our website: www.commfound.org.

CI International is a training and professional development firm that offers consulting, workshops, and coaching solutions to fuel exceptional performance throughout organizations. Our work is focused on creating sustainable change in individuals, teams, and entire organizations, primarily in the government workplace.

Founded on the idea that greatness exists in all of us, helping our clients realize greatness is central to our vision and inherent in our values. Throughout our history our work has been focused on helping our clients:

- Lead more effectively
- Communicate better
- Work more efficiently
- Learn, grow, and thrive personally and professionally

Community giving is ingrained in our culture, inspiring us to not only provide support to organizations in need, but also to share our time, talent and passion by donating our services to the people who need them the most. We sponsor each employee in giving two days per year to a worthy cause. We volunteer with at-risk children and at animal shelters, for Habitat for Humanity, community libraries and churches, among many other deserving causes. We strive to be good tenants of the communities where we live and work. We are honored to be a part of helping the homeless population of Boulder County through this book project.